LETTERS TO SARA

The Agony of Adult Sibling Loss

By

Anne McCurry

ISBN: 0-75966-572-9

This book is printed on acid free paper.

To protect the privacy of the family, the names, locations, ages, professions, and number of children have been changed in this book.

1stBooks - rev. 09/24/01

My only sketch, profile, of Heaven is a large blue sky,
and larger than the biggest I have seen in June—and in
it are my friends—every one of them.

~ Emily Dickinson

Dear Sara—

One month since you died, big sister. Where are you? Did there really turn out to be a Heaven? Did you get in, even though you left the church a long time ago? Were Mom and Dad there to greet you when you got there? How are they? Were they young and healthy, or were they like they were when they died—Dad all ash-gray and skinny, Mom a withered little shadow of herself?

I like to think that when I die, I'll look for all eternity like I did on the best day of my life. No bad hair days, no pot belly. No cellulite or double chin or wrinkles. I hope that's how it is for you. You were always self-conscious about your looks, especially about your weight. Your weight was perfect when you died, and for several months prior to that. But, as you said, cancer was not a diet you would recommend for anyone.

I picture Heaven as a lovely meadow in early spring—fresh as innocence, with lush green grasses stirring in a gentle breeze, a pure blue sky, colorful butterflies and chirping birds flitting about. I envision people and pets that I've loved and lost racing toward me eagerly, arms outstretched in welcome, tails madly wagging. Is that what's it like?

If I didn't think you were someplace like that, I could bear this even less. There's this huge, aching hole in our lives—mine and Joe's and Lisa's. Well, Lisa's and mine, anyway. Joe...I don't know—that husband of yours doesn't act very grief stricken. He displays no outward grief at all. And he's already looking for another woman. My God, it's only been *one month*. You would be heartbroken at how Joe's been carrying on, Sara. None of us can understand it.

He hasn't even had the common good sense to keep his immediate search for a new woman from Lisa. He tells her "life must go on" and "your mom wouldn't want me to be alone" and all that *crap*. Lisa's devastated, of course. A 17-year-old girl isn't going to be eager for her dad to hook up with someone else when her mom—the best mom in the world—has just died.

I feel funny telling you these things—but I guess you know all now, where you are. I've been so upset since I heard what Joe's up to. I don't care what he does with his life, but if it affects Lisa I care a lot. She doesn't need any more suffering of any kind for a long, long time. I hurt for her. I want to hug her and hold her and comfort her. But she's a continent away, in Seattle, while I'm here in upstate New York. And I have to go through Joe to get to her.

Grief teaches the steadiest minds to waver.

~ Sophocles

Dear Sara—

The images, the memories…they overwhelm me. Why is it that no matter how many good years you have with someone you love, no matter how many happy times you've shared, the memories and images that loom largest are the death images and death memories? It's as if death and loss trump anything and everything that's gone before.

Maybe it's not that way for everyone. Maybe it's just me. I do tend to think dark thoughts, dwell on the negative rather than the positive. So unlike you—you were the family's ray of sunshine, a luminous presence that lit up any room you entered. You *glowed*—with life, with love of life, with energy and enthusiasm. Whereas, comparatively, I've always sort of sat in the dark alone. How two sisters sharing the same genes and only a year apart in age could be so different has always mystified me. I guess that's why I used to think I was adopted when I was little. And you, you stinker, told me yes, I probably was.

All I see, awake or asleep, is you lying there dying. I'm obsessed. I know this will eventually lessen. I'm experienced; I've been through other losses—Mom and Dad, Aunt Rose, the cats and dogs and horses that were my "babies," full members of the family. I died a little with each loss, but nothing prepared me for the loss of you, my Sara, my only sibling. Trust me, you don't want to be the surviving sibling. You don't want to be the last survivor of a family.

So much has happened since your death. I want to tell you about these things and laugh and cry with you about them. And a couple of distressing situations have come up where I need your wise advice and counsel so much. And you're not here.

What am I going to do without you?

Hope is a risk that must be run.

~ Georges Bernanos

Dear Sara—

What a struggle your death was...what a fighter you were! Dying was your biggest challenge ever. You would *not* give in to it. You would not once during those three horrible years from diagnosis to death admit that you were dying. Letting go of life was the hardest work you ever did.

And Sara, sweet Sara, that's what made it especially hard. I think it would have been easier for me, for us, for you, if you *had* accepted it, if you had made peace with it. Because death took you by surprise. You looked so frightened, so bewildered, so "this *can't* be happening to me" at the end when your eyes briefly flew open that it was doubly, triply heartbreaking to watch.

All along, you treated breast cancer as though it were a chronic disease that could be controlled indefinitely, even if the controls were terribly unpleasant. When it metastasized to your liver, you just upped the treatments, without complaint. But you never gave in. You expected that there would be another chemo drug that would work for a while, then when that one stopped being effective, there'd be another and then another.... And that did work, for quite a long time.

The handwriting was on the wall from the very beginning, though, with those first awful pathology reports after your surgery. I went to Dr. Goode that week and told her about the path reports. "Sara's going to die, isn't she?" I asked. Dr. Goode looked at me with sweet compassion and nodded her head, saying softly, "Probably."

I started wailing. I screamed, "No! No!" They heard me in the waiting room; I could tell by the way they sneaked embarrassed little glances at me when I left the office. But I couldn't help it. Dr. Goode had confirmed the unimaginable, the unbearable: you were going to die.

I've never known a world without you, Sara. You were already here when I was born.

One cannot live forever by ignoring the price of coffins.

~ Ernest Bramah

Dear Sara—

As you lay dying, we found your last "to do" list, written just a few days earlier. The things on it should have been done months before. They were important, Sara.

You *had* accomplished the two chores that must have held the highest priority for you, though: choosing your gravesite, and setting up your trust. You wanted to pick out your eternal resting-place yourself, just in case the worst did happen. And you wanted to make sure Lisa was protected financially, for the same reason. Good choices, Sara.

You did an excellent job with your burial site. It's beautiful—lovely old trees, a striking view, a stone bench to sit on when we visit you. I'm so pleased that you picked a cemetery with *character*, unlike that dreary place Mom and Dad are buried, with nothing but flat, nearly-anonymous markers on their graves. No matter how often I visit, I have trouble finding them because all parts of that cemetery look alike, as does everyone's grave. It's frustrating and depressing.

You visited your gravesite often during your last couple of months, which struck us as odd because you seemed so certain that you weren't going to die. I can only imagine what going there felt like. To sit and contemplate the spot where your body might soon lie forever...it must have felt surreal, especially since you felt pretty good and stayed fully active to the end. But the medical tests, one after another and closer and closer together, showed cancer out of control, galloping toward the finish line unless the doctors could pull something else out of their hats. Not knowing whether to plan for death or plan for a living future had to have been excruciating.

The most important thing a father can do for his children
is to love their mother.

~ Theodore M. Hesburgh

Dear Sara—

I talked to Lisa last night—a good, long talk. I had to speak with Joe first, of course, because he answered the phone when I called. I make myself be pleasant to him because he's the gatekeeper for Lisa; if I alienate him, he can make it difficult for me to communicate with her.

Joe must have left the room while Lisa talked with me, or maybe she was on the portable phone and wandered away from him as we spoke, because she was very open. She said she was angry and hurt and confused by her dad's acting so unaffected by your death. She had expected that he would be inconsolable after you died, and that they would help each other through their grief. Nothing of the sort has happened, and she feels very alone in her pain. She is, of course, especially devastated by the sounds he's been making about dating and maybe even re-marrying.

What could I say? Yes, your father *is* a prick, he *is* absolutely being disloyal to your mom's memory? I couldn't do that. Her dad is all she has left. I just made soothing sounds and let her vent. I mumbled something about how different people grieve in different ways.

You know what breaks my heart the most about how Joe's acting? That Lisa might come to think that his behavior is the normal behavior of a grieving spouse. And it's not, not at all. If Lisa thinks it is, how will she ever be able to trust that a relationship is what it seems to be? She, like you, believed that Joe loved you, believed that you were together for life by mutual choice. As if her world weren't shattered enough by your death, now she has to re-adjust how she's always looked at you two as a couple, as her parents. A double earthquake.

Your friends are still coming around a lot, still very concerned and helpful. You would be pleased at how wonderful they've been. They call, they stop by, they bring casseroles (mostly lasagna, still), they take Lisa out to lunch and to the movies. Then they e-mail me and tell me how shocked they are by Joe's apparent lack of grief. It's too bad he can't at least *pretend*, but that's not the way he is. What you see is what you get with Joe, like it or not.

*And in the end it's not the years in your life that count.
It's the life in your years.*

~ Abraham Lincoln

Dear Sara—

I don't imagine Joe will have much trouble finding someone else, if he's really serious in his pursuit. He's still young looking. He's in good shape, and he can be quite charming when he makes the effort. And he has money now, thanks to you.

You told me a few months before you died that you expected Joe would marry again if this cancer did kill you. But your tone was hurt and a little resentful when you said it. Then you laughed and said, "I'm just pissed that I won't be here to see it!" I believed you; you hated to miss out on *anything*.

I've never known anyone so hungry for life as you. You grabbed every opportunity and every experience and savored it. You filled every moment of your life with people and travel and projects and sports and books and music and gardening and, of course, your family and career. If there's any consolation at all in losing you this young, it's that you packed about 85 years of living into your 54. Even before you got cancer, you lived every day as though it were your last.   You were carpe diem personified.

I used to think you were crazy to live life at such a frantic pace, but now I'm glad you did. Or I *think* I'm glad you did. Sometimes I wonder…did you die this young because you wore yourself out with the pace of your life, or did you go at that pace because you sensed you'd die relatively young?

*At the worst, a house unkept cannot be so distressing as
a life unlived.*

~ Rose Macaulay

Dear Sara—

Joe called me today. He asked me to fly out and spend a
week with him to help him clean out the house. He said every
room is full of your "stuff," and that there are pictures of you
everywhere. He wants to pack everything up. Of *course* there
are possessions of yours and pictures of you all around the
house—you lived there 24 years! You married Joe in that house,
raised your child there and then died there.

I was evasive with Joe when he asked me to come, but
managed to get across to him that my answer was "No." How
dare he try to erase you so quickly! And doesn't Lisa have
anything to say about removing all signs of her mom from the
house? I can't imagine she's ready for that.

Okay, your house *is* a mess, and it will indeed be hard for
Joe to get it cleaned out by himself. But that's tough. Maybe
doing it will start him thinking, will make him confront some of
the good memories—and there *were* many, I know there were—
of a life shared with you. Maybe he'll even cry, finally.

He'll probably just hire someone to come in and clean out the house for him, if he can't talk any other woman he knows into helping him. No smart woman would touch that job with a ten-foot pole, though. What a recipe for disaster! Whoever does it will, I suspect, earn the eternal resentment of Lisa, whether that's rational on her part or not. Judging from what Lisa told me, the atmosphere in your home right now is too fraught with tension to make any big decisions—especially any that might seem an attempt to negate your existence. My advice to Joe on the phone yesterday was that, if he felt he had to do it, to save anything and everything of family interest and put it all in storage for Lisa for when she's settled into her own home one day.

It'll be a huge job. You were three of the messiest people and biggest pack rats I've ever seen in my life! It's funny, but good housekeeping, or the lack of it, seems to be a tone set primarily by the woman of the household, even today. It just wasn't one of your priorities, and never was. Living was, and work and activities and friends were. Here again, we're so different; I can't function unless things are clean and orderly and organized around me. You seemed to flourish in disorganization, as though it were the badge of a busy and happy life. Maybe it is.

I know you resented that it was assumed that a neat and orderly house was your responsibility, especially since you were always the main breadwinner of the family. I remember your saying that if Lisa and Joe didn't give a shit about keeping things picked up, why should you? They both had more free time and far fewer responsibilities than you did.

What I didn't tell Joe when he called, and what I'm not going to tell Lisa yet, is that I don't plan on visiting your home ever again. I can't, Sara. You *were* that home, and that home was you. I could not bear to walk in and for you not to be there. I'll phone and e-mail Lisa regularly. She can come east to visit me or we can meet somewhere else for little vacations and get-togethers, reunions. But I can't go to your house without you there.

Do you remember the plaque I have in my kitchen that says, "A home without a dog is just a house"? Well, to me your home without you is no longer a home. It's just a house, but one with incredibly powerful memories, filled with your invisible presence no matter what Joe does to try and eliminate that.

Anne McCurry

Death leaves a heartache no one can heal,
Love leaves a memory no one can steal.

~ From a headstone in Ireland

Dear Sara—

God, so many, many random thoughts. One is that I'm eternally grateful for the fact that we always said, "I love you" at the end of every phone call. Not just after you got cancer, but always, our entire adult lives. And you would make two quick little kissing sounds after saying it. I'll never hear that again.

Another thought is about "closure." I wonder who ever came up with that concept? Or even the word? It must have been someone who hadn't experienced grief. The concept of closure suggests that there's a certain defined point at which you jump up and proclaim, "All better!" and go about your life. No, no, no. Grief is a complex process of varying lengths and strengths for different people. Very gradual. There's a hole, a void, that can never be entirely filled when someone you love dies. I still have holes for Mom and Dad, and they died 20-plus years ago. You try and fill that void as best you can, but it's always there, even if it gets smaller with time. It never fully closes.

One more thought: I do so regret that I didn't get a small piece of your beautiful silver hair before they removed your body from the house. I had fully intended to do that, had thought of doing it for months. And then I forgot in the emotionality of that hour. I was going to find an old mourning brooch or ring, put your hair in it and wear it always, a physical part of you that would be with me. I am *so* mad at myself for forgetting.

I was reading the other night that for a time in the early 18th century, Americans who lost loved ones would provide each guest at the funeral with a pair of black gloves and a mourning ring. I wish we still did things like that. I wish we still wore black for a year after someone close to us dies. I would happily do that. It would proclaim to the world that I am suffering, I am grieving—don't try to cheer me up, give me time, let me work through my grief. I saw a T-shirt on eBay that had "Leave Me Alone" written across the chest in big, black letters, and I was tempted....

I was grateful that any of us who wanted to could put a little something special in your coffin with you. I cut a lock of my own hair, tied it with a purple ribbon and put it in the little bagful of mementos that was taken to the mortuary. So even if I don't have a lock of your hair—although "lock" isn't the right word, your hair was so very short at the end—you have a lock of mine with you for all eternity. I feel good about that.

And I feel good that my hair was its natural color! I wouldn't have put an artificially-colored piece of my hair in with you, you who loved all things natural. I'm glad I finally decided to quit coloring my hair and let it grow out. Do you remember that time at my dining room table when Aunt Carol leaned forward and asked me, in front of everybody, if that was my natural hair color? Then she leaned back, the bitch, and said, "Never mind—we'll love you through this color, as we have through all the others." I reached the point where I realized that since all the women in our family had very attractive silver or sparkling white hair as they aged, I probably would too. And sure enough, mine's not bad. I like it.

You can clutch the past so tightly to your chest that it leaves your arms too full to embrace the present.

~ Jan Glidewell

Dear Sara—

I obsess about Joe. I need to understand why he's acting like he is, why he appears to feel no grief whatsoever.

I've started researching grief on the Internet and, my God, it's a *huge* subject! But I've already learned a lot, and it's helping. It keeps me busy and distracted and interested in something, rather than going through life like a zombie, as I've been doing for so long now.

Dr. Goode says I've been in a "state of being," a state of just existing while waiting helplessly for you to die. I've been "stuck," unable to do much of anything since your diagnosis. I felt I had to be always available in case you needed me to rush out to you in a hurry. I literally didn't plan anything more than a week in advance during the entire last year of your life.

And I still feel paralyzed, even now that you're dead, isn't that odd? It's probably a matter of not accepting your death yet. It's hard to believe that you're really gone, that you truly did die. I know for a fact that you did; I was there. But you always loomed so huge in my life, big sister, you were literally so larger-than-life to me that I've had trouble accepting that you are no longer here. I've been tied in knots for so long, consumed with sick worry about your every symptom, that I have to remind myself many times a day that you're gone. That there's nothing more to worry about, because it's *over* now. That there's nothing more I can do to help you. I tell myself that, over and over again. But it doesn't sink in.

Maybe if there'd been some sort of religious aspect surrounding your death it would seem more real, more final: a pastor making a final visit to bless you and shore us up, a priest reading the last rites. Sitting Shiva, in the Jewish tradition, would have been particularly helpful, I think. To stop all normal activities for seven intense days and do nothing but think and talk of you, to concentrate on nothing but you and having lost you seems like it would immerse one in the reality of the loss and give a good and healthy start toward acceptance. I wish we could have done that. It sounds like a custom that wouldn't *let* one delay or deny or escape grief, which has to be better in the long run.

I also like the idea, again in the Jewish tradition, of rending garments, tearing your clothing as a symbol of a broken heart. That would have felt good, would have felt right. I appreciate customs, and think they might have helped. Your ceremony was lovely, but it lacked any traditions or rituals. It was very ad-lib. But maybe that was appropriate for a free spirit like you.

One Jewish ritual that you yourself liked, though, and that you got me doing, was the lighting of Yahrtzeit candles that burn for 24 hours for special anniversaries of those we'd loved and lost. We lit them for Mom and Dad, on the anniversaries of their birthdays and death days. Those little ceremonies meant a lot to you, as they now do to me. Strictly speaking, I think they're supposed to be lit only for the death anniversary, but we did it for birthdays too. They're supposed to be lit at sunset the night before the anniversary day, but we lit them the morning of. I'll light one for you at sunset the night before the anniversary of your death, so it will go out right at sunset the next day, commemorating the exact moment of your passing. I will be lighting Yahrtzeit candles for you as long as I live or as long as I have memory, Sara.

I had a dream about you last night. It wasn't a ghostly-visitation kind of dream, just you doing ordinary things. I don't know what it means. I haven't slept well since you died, and have had almost no dreams that I'm able to remember.

*Regret for the things we did can be tempered by time; it
is regret for the things we did not do that is
inconsolable.*

~ Sidney J. Harris

Dear Sara—

I think that what Joe is experiencing is something called
"complicated" grief, also known as "pathological" grief. That's
what I'm learning in my grief research. Mostly those terms refer
to people who experience chronic grief—grief that just doesn't
stop even after a long period of time. Those people are stuck in
the grieving process, and the pain never lessens.

But one form of complicated grief is "absent" grief.
Evidently it's relatively rare, but it happens. It's when grief and
any sort of mourning process are totally absent. That's Joe, all
right. I read that "the existence of a highly ambivalent
relationship to the deceased" is a risk factor for absent grief.
Well, yeah, I admit that your marriage sometimes struck me as a
love/hate relationship, on both sides. But until the last few
months of your life, I believed that Joe honestly loved you, when
all was said and done. I know you loved him, in spite of your
differences; you said it and you showed it.

An absence of grief is a sign of danger, according to one website. The person experiencing absent grief can end up with medical symptoms or display "aberrant behavior." Hmmm. Joe has always been a hypochondriac. Even though your medical appointments and procedures were almost constant these past few years, I remember you telling me that *he* actually had more doctor appointments than you did—and there was nothing wrong with him! I wonder if he'll start having all sorts of psychosomatic illnesses now.

I read that when a marriage has been filled with conflict, the surviving spouse can feel a "rueful gratification" at now being able to decide things without argument. Maybe this is the price you're both paying for your being the dominant one and Joe the passive one in the marriage. I don't know. I thought he liked it that way. You were the one with strength and direction, never Joe. You pretty much called all the shots, but that was because he wouldn't or couldn't. You were the mover and the shaker; Joe was the go-alonger. He seemed to have no ability to make friends of his own, and he had no particular ambitions. Granted, he's been an exceptionally good father, but his main identity seemed to be that of "Sara's husband." Just as much of my own identity has been that of "Sara's sister."

I guess we both have to reinvent ourselves now.

A sister is both your mirror—and your opposite.

~ Elizabeth Fishel

Dear Sara—

Studying grief is turning out to be enormously helpful. All my feelings are normal, which I think I knew, but it's nice to have it validated. The so-called stages of grief don't count for much, though—I go back and forth between denial, anger, sadness, yearning, and disbelief like a yo-yo in the hands of an amateur. I suspect most people do—there's probably no one-two-three about it for anyone.

I'm finding surprisingly little information about, or help in dealing with, adult sibling loss, though. There's plenty about spousal loss and parental loss and about children who lose a sibling, but not much about adult sibling loss. That's odd, because it's such a *major* loss. There is no one more like you in the world than a sibling. It's a relationship that lasts from childhood to death, literally spanning the entire course of a lifetime. Sometimes it's the *only* relationship that lasts that long. Siblings share a unique mix of intimacy, biology and childhood experiences that you'll never have with anyone else on earth.

Siblings start out by being stuck with each other, since there's not usually much choice about living in the same home with your brothers and sisters and sharing the same parents. Sibs practice life on one another—learning how to negotiate, how to communicate, how to compromise. It's *good* that you're stuck with one another, because it forces you to learn to interact with others. If a friend gets upset with you, she can flounce out of your life in a huff, never to return. But a sibling can't. She has to stay and learn how to work things out.

I had assumed that the strongest sibling bond of all is the bond between sisters. In fact, I just read that the bond can be so intense that it rivals even a mother-daughter bond. But I've learned in my visits to online grief chatrooms that adult brother/brother and adult brother/sister bonds can be just as powerful; the pain of those I've chatted with who have lost brothers is every bit as terrible as mine at losing you.

*The web of our life is of a mingled yarn, good and ill
together.*

~ William Shakespeare

Dear Sara—

What tears me apart, what breaks my heart, what *haunts* me
is that Joe might have been intentionally cruel to you at the end,
when you were helpless. I've pieced this together from things
Joe said to me a couple of months before you died, and things he
said to me just after you died.

Before that time, I'd had no real worries on that score. I
knew he had some issues with your being a little controlling over
the years, but he is such a non-assertive person that I thought he
probably appreciated a strong helpmate. I assumed he adored
you, as we all did, no matter what your faults. What you offered
the world in compassionate advice on your radio show, and the
totally non-judgmental attitude you had toward anyone and
everyone in your life made you so special that any little personal
quirks were overlooked by all. At least that was my assumption.
In every person, you have to weigh the good against the bad, and
the checkmarks on the good side of the board outnumbered the
bad by 100 to one in your case.

I had appreciated that Joe was by your side taking care of you during these last years. When he and I had talked during that time, I'd felt real sadness, real regret, from him whenever we talked about your prognosis. He cried a couple of times. He claimed you were his best friend, really his only friend. He spoke of the future you two would never have together. I was grateful you had him.

Then everything changed, and I don't know why. When I visited you two months before you died, Joe seemed angry and resentful toward you, even mocking. He said things like, "Why won't she admit she's dying? Why does she refuse to prepare for it?" He said it in a tone of voice that implied you were a fool to be optimistic, an ostrich with your head buried in the sand. I was surprised, since I felt—and thought he did too—that your amazingly optimistic attitude is what had gotten you so far in your battle with breast cancer. Certainly your doctors thought so.

Then Joe said, "She lies there in bed, calling out orders like a little dictator: 'Bring me this, get me that, I need…whatever….' I don't know if that's because of the cancer, or if it's just Sara being Sara."

Well, that shocked me down to my toes. How could he say that about his desperately ill wife? If he were in your shoes, he'd be bedridden some of the time too. He'd be reduced to asking for help occasionally. If he'd just gotten home from yet another debilitating chemo session, he wouldn't be expected to hop up and fix himself a sandwich. He'd have to ask for help.

When I got back home, I had a whole session with Dr. Goode about Joe's changed attitude. I was *so* alarmed, so worried for you. I'd gotten the feeling that he was in a state of terrible impatience for you to die. What would that mean for you?

Dr. Goode advised me to call and sound you out, to see if you'd noticed a change in Joe or felt you were being mistreated in any way. So I called you and chatted about other things for a while, then casually asked if people were "being good to you." You sounded puzzled and asked, "What do you mean?" I said, "Oh...Joe and Lisa and everyone—are they being good to you, kind to you?"

In a shocked voice, you answered, "Oh, yes!" So I let it drop. With some trepidation, I wrote it off to the tremendous stress and strain of taking care of someone you love who is terminally ill.

But my intuition was right. Within an hour of your death, Joe sat beside me and started poor-mouthing you. He seemed energized, almost hyperactive, very different from his usual self. He said, "Sara's life is over. Now *my* life can begin."

Imagine saying that to me, your sister who adored you and whose heart had truly just broken? I listened in numbed shock. He told me that he doubted you two would ever have stayed together if it weren't for Lisa. I know he said other things too, but I honestly can't remember them. Things that happened and were said in those first hours after you died are hazy in my mind, other than those first two comments of Joe's. It must have been overload—I tuned him out after that. My emotions could deal with nothing more.

Cruelty, like every other vice, requires no motive outside
of itself; it only requires opportunity.

~ George Eliot

Dear Sara—

I'm beginning to think that because you were such an exceptionally tolerant and forgiving person it could be you who's leading me to research various kinds of grief so that I'll understand about Joe.

I didn't sleep much last night. Writing yesterday about Joe's attitude toward you at the end got me all stirred up again. I have to continue until I get it out of my system. Maybe I'll gain some perspective if I see the facts on paper, rather than swirling around chaotically in my head. I have a terrible need to talk to you about these things, and this is the only way I can think of to communicate with you.

By the time I arrived at your house, less than two days before you died, you'd already been unconscious for a few hours, so we were never able to talk together. But what I've been able to piece together from others' accounts of your last couple of conscious days breaks my heart. I learned that two days before you lost consciousness, you and Joe went to the park for a short walk and then sat in the sun and talked. Joe himself told me that he talked to you about how unhappy he'd been in the marriage. What cruelty, what *cowardice*, to wait until you were totally helpless and dependent on him, until you were literally within days of death to tell you that! And what a shock for you to hear it, because I know you believed that Joe loved you and had been, all in all, happy with you.

I heard from your good friend Janis that you were terribly agitated the next day, your last full day of consciousness. She said you called her four times and just sobbed, unable to form the words to tell her what you wanted. Your mental confusion had gotten awfully bad by then, as your bilirubin counts skyrocketed. How terrifying not being able to find words must have been for someone like you, who had always been so remarkably gifted with words.

After Janis told me about the phone calls to her, I asked Joe what he thought that might have been about. It was important to me to know what you were thinking. That's when he told me about your talk in the park. He said that you'd been calling Janis to ask her for help in composing a letter to him, but that you were too confused to put it into words.

What would you have said in that letter, Sara? Joe had a self-righteous tone when he told me of the talk in the park and your attempt to write a letter to him. He seemed to assume that it was to have been a letter of apology for making his life miserable and gratitude for his taking care of you throughout your illness. Is that what it would have been? I have no idea, and I want *so* much to know. But I never will; that's a mystery you took to the grave with you.

What I fear is that you endured great mental anguish at the end. Not only at the realization, finally, that this cancer really was going to kill you, and soon, but at the realization that your life had not been what you believed it to be.

How can I ever forgive Joe?

Because I could not stop for death,
He kindly stopped for me.
The carriage held but just ourselves
And Immortality.

~ Emily Dickinson

Dear Sara—

Joe did see that I got there in time. I'm grateful to him for that. My flight was a late one, and it was midnight when I walked into your house. You were in a hospital bed supplied just hours earlier by Hospice. You were motionless, eyes closed, mouth open, breathing erratically.

I took your hand and said, "Sara, it's Anne. I'm here." Your eyes half-opened, then closed again. I stayed on the floor all night next to the bed, one arm up, my hand holding yours. You stopped breathing several times in the night, but then started again. Lisa and Janis were there too, sprawled around the room, resting as best they could. Joe stayed in his own bed and slept.

You made it through that night and the next, but your breathing became more ragged as time passed, and a rattle started in your throat. The Hospice people came back and inserted a catheter. They monitored your blood pressure, which was sinking lower and lower. But you fought on. You wouldn't let go.

We all talked to you, giving you permission to leave us. Your struggle was horrible to watch, and we encouraged you to go. You were never alone. You were constantly stroked and talked to and held. Lisa crawled into the bed with you. She took you in her arms, murmuring "Mommy, Mommy."

You never spoke or seemed to recognize any of us. Your eyes briefly flew open a few times, and I thought I saw fear and wonder and confusion in your fixed stare. Other than that, your eyes were alternately closed or half-open and unseeing, responding to nothing, occasionally oozing tears. When we'd turn you, your body was heavy and floppy, totally helpless. And yet your neck was as rigid as a log.

There was no incontinence of any kind, no messes, no odors. Your person was as neat and clean as death approached as you could ever have hoped for. You looked surprisingly good, except that you were very yellow and you were a little bloated around your tummy. You weren't at all "wasted-looking." You looked like a woman in great shape who was unaccountably dying. I couldn't believe you really were. I half-expected you to sit up and laugh and say, "What's going on? You all act like I'm dying or something!" Which were, of course, the very words you had used in our last conversation together.

The second day was beautiful—mild and sunny. You were still fighting, hanging on against all odds. I had a feeling—which grew stronger and stronger as the hours passed—that you needed to be outside to die, you who loved nature above all else and who couldn't stand to be indoors on a nice day. I kept urging the others to get you outdoors, and they finally agreed that we would all wheel the bed out into the back yard. We did, and you immediately seemed more peaceful. We tucked your favorite comforter around you and even protected your eyes by putting your sunglasses on. You were bathed one last time in the sunshine you so loved.

There was an exquisite sunset that evening, and you died exactly at the moment that the sun set. We were all with you, touching you, telling you we loved you. It was a lovely time to die. Never again will any of us see a beautiful sunset without thinking of you. Good timing, Sara.

When they came from the mortuary to remove your body, Janis made Joe and Lisa and me go into Lisa's bedroom and stay a while. How wise that turned out to be! It would have been extremely difficult to see you leave your beloved home for the last time, never to return. I'm grateful for her sensitivity.

Down, down, down into the darkness of the grave.
Gently they go, the beautiful, the tender, the kind;
Quickly they go, the intelligent, the witty, the brave.
I know. But I do not approve. And I am not resigned.

~ Edna St. Vincent Millay

Dear Sara—

I have to admit Joe did a good job with your funeral. Since you'd prepared for death only insofar as to pick out your gravesite, there was a lot to do. He jumped right in and organized it all. Here again, so different from his usual lethargic self.

He called lots of people who, in turn, called others. He chose the music for the service. He picked out the coffin and the headstone, although that won't be ready for a while. He wrote an obituary with help from your friends and co-workers, since none of us could remember all of your educational and professional credits and awards. The paper ran a big obituary, with a photo of you and quotes from Joe and some of your friends in the business.

I was surprised to find that you hadn't written an obit yourself ahead of time. Remember how impressed we were with

34

the one Aunt Rose had written, ready and waiting when the time came? We both thought that was a wonderful idea, because how can you know what people want said about themselves, what areas of their lives they'd like to highlight in their death notices or obituaries, if they don't tell you or write it themselves?

Lisa and I picked out your burial outfit, the periwinkle two-piece that you liked so well. I hope that was all right. We included matching jewelry, of course. You always looked so well put together, we thought it was important that you have a coordinated outfit. Periwinkle was definitely your color, with your blue eyes and silver hair.

There were *hundreds* of people at your burial. There was even a TV crew for a while and, of course, your radio station had someone there reporting. The service was held outside at the cemetery, right by your coffin. You, the outdoor girl, would have liked that. The weather held, thankfully.

Since you had no religious affiliation, anyone who wanted to say or read something was encouraged to. And it seemed that almost everyone did! We were there for hours. It was wonderful…you were probably blushing in Heaven at all the nice things that were said about you. The atmosphere overall was undeniably sad. We cried and we hugged, but we also laughed a little at some of the stories your friends told about you. People read poems or just talked about you. A couple of women chose to sing songs to you. You clearly were a person who made a strong impression on others.

The best part of your service was the doves. Joe arranged to rent pure-white homing doves for the family to release at the end of the service. Their soft cooing as they waited patiently in their crates was soothing during the long ceremony, as though nature itself had gentle things to say about you. I thought they were going to be released all at once at the conclusion of the service but, no, each family member was handed one to carefully hold.

We each took a dove, and we circled your coffin, which was still aboveground. The doves were big and healthy and squirmy.

It wasn't all that easy to hold onto them without hurting them, but we did it. We stood holding them for a few minutes, calling out our last messages and good-byes to you. Then we counted to three and released them. It was magnificent! They immediately banded together, and then they swooped and swirled for quite a long while, pure white against the brilliant blue sky, before getting their bearings and heading home.

What a way to end a funeral! We all had big smiles on our faces. How you would have enjoyed the drama and beauty of the doves! The best thing about it, of course, is that Lisa's main memory of her mom's funeral will not be that of doom and gloom, but of something very special and beautiful.

Everyone left before your casket was lowered into the ground.

*Mourning is not forgetting... it is an undoing. Every
minute tie has to be untied and something permanent
and valuable recovered and assimilated from the dust.*

~ Margery Allingham

Dear Sara—

I flew home late that night, the night of your burial. I
couldn't wait to get out of that Sara-less house and back to my
own quiet home, to grieve in peace. I'd been there a week, and
had had more than my fill of chaos and discomfort and people,
people everywhere. I'd slept on the floor at your house the
whole time I was there, first because I wanted to be near you all
night and then, after you died, because Joe's family descended
and needed beds.

I remember virtually nothing of the flights home. I seem to
have put myself in a trance, so that I wouldn't break down until I
safely closed the door of my house behind me. To say I was
glad to get home is an understatement. But I came home to
reality—to a life without you. And I'm not looking forward to
that.

My Tim has been wonderfully sweet and considerate to me
since you died. He can see how much I'm hurting. But he's

never lost anyone he loved, remarkably enough, so he doesn't fully understand the pain and turmoil of a loss. Thank God I've got Dr. Goode and a grief chatroom I found online and, now, these letters to you to help me. Doing the letters wasn't a conscious decision on my part—I just sat down one day and began writing to you. I *had* to find some way to "talk" to you, to tell you of my agony at losing you and about how upset I am at Joe's behavior.

Unless you die very young—or you're exceptionally lucky, like Tim—everyone everywhere in the world experiences grief in his or her lifetime. I think the first experience anyone has with grief, though, is the worst—you have nothing with which to compare such pain, and grief can be so intense and multi-faceted that you think you might be losing your mind.

I came across a story involving the Buddha and a woman's first experience with grief. Her name was Kisagotami, and she and her wealthy husband had one child, a boy. When the boy was a toddler, he got very sick and died. Kisagotami could not accept his death. She carried the little boy's body from house to house, begging for medicine to bring her baby back to life. Someone finally took pity on her, and told her to go see the Buddha, that he might have medicine to help the boy. She rushed to the Buddha, who told her that she must procure a small amount of mustard seed for the supposed cure, *but* that she had to get it from a house that had never known death. Still carrying her dead child, Kisagotami went door to door on her task, only to find that there was not a single household that had not known death. This showed her the universality of death, and that death is part of the nature of life. She regained her senses and buried her boy in the woods.

Death and grief are painful in all cultures, as far as I know. In the research I've been doing, I read that the Neanderthals stained their dead with red ochre, which seems to demonstrate special feelings and treatment for those of their kind who died. And I know for a fact that animals mourn. Remember when the neighbor's cocker spaniel was run over and killed by the milk truck in front of our house? And our dog Snoopy, who was great buddies with the cocker, walked to that spot hours later and threw back his head and howled and howled? He did that several days running. We ourselves didn't know for a couple of days that the cocker had been killed there.

There is no healthy way to avoid grieving when someone you love dies—not if you hope to come out the other side and recover. Although I'm not sure there's really a "recovery" from grief any more than there is true "closure." The best word I can think of to describe the final result of working through grief is *adaptation*; you manage to adapt to a world without the loved one you lost. Somehow you have to learn to adapt. It can't be rushed; it takes as long as it takes. One day at a time. Baby steps. Although some days it seems to be one step forward and two steps backwards.

My emotions run the gamut of many of the worst, most-avoided human feelings: rage, fear, denial, disbelief, pain, guilt, yearning, despair, depression. But I know I have to feel them. As author John Gray says, "What you feel, you can heal." Avoidance or denial or postponement will all come back to bite you, even worse than if you'd grieved in the first place.

Sara, you were my sister, my best friend, my hero, my role model, my confidante. We had our share of differences when we were growing up, but it's funny how they seemed to disappear when we became adults. I feel blessed that we had the time to talk about any and all past problems or misunderstandings, apologize for them and forgive each other wholeheartedly.

Remember the last words you spoke to me face-to-face two months before you died, when you dropped me off at the airport? Even though neither one of us had admitted that you were going to die, you turned to me and said, "Now, is there anything still unresolved between us? Is there anything more we need to say?" I said no, that I thought everything had been said and resolved.

Then we hugged each other for the last time although, of course, we didn't know it was for the last time.

We were so lucky to have had the time to talk. Imagine if either of us had been killed in an accident or murdered or had a sudden, fatal heart attack or something—we wouldn't have gotten to say goodbye and resolve anything from the past. The sudden loss of someone you love, especially in a senseless or violent way, has to be the worst kind of loss. Trauma is piled upon the grief to such an extent that it must take much, much longer to work through, if you ever do. Yes, we were very fortunate to be granted both forewarning and time.

I've been reading about grief resolution, and discover that I'm not even past the first step: accept the reality of the loss. I haven't been able to yet. The second step, broadly speaking, is to work through the pain and the grief. I've got a long way to go on that one. Next is to adjust to an environment in which the deceased is missing. Well, I guess I don't have much choice about that.

Last is to "emotionally relocate" the deceased and move on with life. What does that mean? Physically, I've gradually been able to stop thinking about you in your earthly home in Seattle and think of you as being in Heaven. But where—and how—am I supposed to relocate you emotionally? Another way of describing this last step is "to withdraw emotional energy and reinvest it," meaning withdraw emotional energy from you and reinvest it in someone else. Who? I will never have another sister.

The thing is, I don't know that I *want* the grieving process to end. Wouldn't that be disloyal to you? Even though we never directly addressed *your* death, we talked about various aspects of death in general, and I know for a fact that your biggest fear was that of being forgotten. You were afraid that no one would remember you after a while.

Sara, I doubt that anyone who crossed your path in life will forget you. Especially will I never forget you in my lifetime, nor

Lisa in hers. Mostly that's due to who and what you were. But it's also because of all those videos of you and Lisa that Joe took over the years, and because of that wonderful "book" you wrote to Lisa—the story of your life that you combined with our family history, along with all sorts of loving advice for her future. Lisa hasn't been able to bring herself to read it yet, but she will be blown away by it, I know she will. She will be tremendously grateful to have that in years to come, and will pass it down to future generations.

Anne McCurry

> *Our memories are an untidy family album crammed with*
> *images and dreams, scattered and uncatalogued, and*
> *their sudden recurrence is wholly unpredictable.*

> ~ Don Freeman

Dear Sara—

Because we were so close in age, Mom dressed us as twins. You *hated* that, but I liked it; anything that identified me even more with you was great with me. You were my hero.

Even though you were only a year older, you were more of a mother to me than Mom was. I was extraordinarily dependent on you. You were a natural-born leader, and I was a natural-born follower. And now you've led the way in death. It's funny, but dying is not nearly as scary to me now that you've gone first. You'll be there to help me through it and welcome me to the hereafter.

Mom was a driven kind of personality, like you. She was too busy working and socializing and being president of this organization and treasurer of that club to have a whole lot of time for us. You vowed to avoid being that kind of mother, and you succeeded. No matter what myriad of activities you were caught up in, you still managed to be a committed, involved mother to Lisa. Motherhood was sacred to you. But you paid a high price for it; superb mothering added to everything else you felt you had to accomplish to perfection wore you out. I swear, you were *born* burning the candle at both ends, and you can get away with that for only so long before it meets in the middle and extinguishes itself.

You gave 110 percent to anything you committed yourself to. Anyone who knew you could attest to that. You were the most responsible, dependable person I've ever known. You could be counted upon to be where you were supposed to be, when you were supposed to be there, doing what you were supposed to be doing. You had tremendously strong work and commitment ethics. If you said you'd do something, you'd do it, come hell or high water.

Except that one time.... I'll never forget the one time you didn't show up when you were supposed to. It was when you and the aunts came to our place for a short visit, a mini-reunion, five summers ago. Tim and I somehow found room to put both Aunt Rose and Aunt Carol up here—always a challenge because they insisted on separate rooms wherever they went—and you stayed at the Marriott about 15 minutes away.

While you were in town, I'd arranged for us to have a tour of the house we grew up in, remember? We had to be there at 10:00 on a Saturday morning; you were to come here at 9:00, and we'd take our time driving over to our old house. Nine o'clock came and went. Then 9:15. The aunts and I sat around drinking coffee and chatting as we waited for you, but I was becoming anxious. It wasn't like you to be late. In fact, I'd *never* known you to be late for anything. By 9:30, I began to seriously worry. What if you'd had an accident driving over? I finally snatched up the phone and called the hotel, giving the switchboard your room number.

A woman's groggy voice answered on the second ring, and I immediately began apologizing. I felt terrible at having awakened some innocent traveler.

"I'm *so* sorry!" I said. "They must have put me through to the wrong room. I'm trying to reach my sister; she was supposed to be at my place a half-hour ago. I was calling room 235."

"This is room 235," the sleepy voice said.

"Well, I don't understand it," I babbled on. "She said that was her room number."

"What time is it?" the voice mumbled.

"A little after 9:30,"

"Oh, my God!" the woman exclaimed, sounding much more alert. "The front desk called and woke me at 8:00, but I must have fallen back asleep! I'm late!"

"Well," I said cheerily, still embarrassed but feeling much less guilty, "maybe it's a good thing I *did* get the wrong number, since you meant to get up earlier! Do you think you could reconnect me with the front desk, so I can track down my sister?"

"*Anne*," the voice said, "this *is* your sister! I went back to sleep by mistake!"

"*Sara?*" I said in disbelief. "You *can't* be Sara! Sara's supposed to be *here*."

"Ahhh!" you said in exasperation. "I'll throw some clothes on and be there as soon as I can! Call them to tell them we'll be late." You slammed the phone down.

I stood staring stupidly at the receiver for a few moments, and then called the folks who were letting us tour their house. At first I was mad; how could you let me down, making me call those kind people to tell them we'd be late? They'd gotten up early on a Saturday morning to show us their house when they didn't have to. But I soon saw the humor, and I've laughed myself silly about it many times since. It was so totally inconceivable to me that you not be somewhere when you said you would be that I was literally unable to recognize your voice. That woman who'd overslept *could not* be my sister and therefore *was not* my sister. That's how strong a reputation for rock-solid dependability you had.

Mom was not dependable, was she? How many times was she late picking us up from lessons or after-school activities when we were kids? Too many to count. Sometimes she would forget to get us at all. In my photo album, I have a picture of us waiting for Mom—two forlorn-looking little girls sitting on a busy street curb, cheeks bulging with lollipops, waiting to be picked up.

No, during our childhood it was you and me alone, trying to find our places in the world. You'd take me shopping for clothes and decide what I could and couldn't buy. You'd make me go to church with you every Sunday, back in the days when you believed with a passion. You decided what after-school activities we would get involved in. You were a little tyrant!

Yet, oddly enough, *I* always felt strongly protective of *you*. And it had nothing to do with the fact that you were petite and I was so big. In spite of your powerful personality and your obvious strengths, there was always a vulnerability and a fragility about you. When I was young, I would sometimes awaken in the night crying, terrified that you were going to die and leave me all alone. And now you have. My worst childhood nightmare has come true.

*Great opportunities to help others seldom come, but
small ones come daily.*

~ Ivy Baker Priest

Dear Sara—

I remember that whenever one of us was sick and had to stay home from school, Mom would make us both stay home. She had to work and couldn't stay with us, but she didn't want either one of us to be home alone. The well one of the two of us had to take care of the sick one.

And that's how it's been these past few years, hasn't it? I've been the well one and you've been the sick one, and there's been nothing I wouldn't do to help you. I offered you my blood and part of my own liver, to try and buy more time. But you and the doctors said it wouldn't do any good. I'd have exchanged my life for yours if I could have.

I flew out to be with you so many times that I lost count. I think and hope I was a real help to you. There were things you wanted done, and you weren't good at accomplishing projects. I am, so that worked out well. We re-planted your gardens together and redecorated your living room and cleaned out your attic—all those things that would have overwhelmed you had you tried to do them alone, but that you really wanted done. I feel good about those projects.

Anne McCurry

*The only way to keep your health is to eat what you
don't want, drink what you don't like and do what you'd
rather not.*

~ Mark Twain

Dear Sara—

What I don't understand about your illness and death
is…why *you*? Why not *me*? From the time you were first
diagnosed, I felt guilty that this had happened to you and not me.
You, who were so much more deserving of life than I because
you made a real contribution to the world, an impact for the
better on others' lives. Whereas I don't do much of anything.

The unfairness overwhelms me. It's like some weird cosmic
mistake that the good sister should die first. I've been reading
about "survivor's guilt," so I know it's not unusual to feel some
guilt that I survived and you didn't. But in this case I think I'm
fully justified in believing it should have been me and not you.

The other grossly unfair aspect of your death is that you
were the one who took exceptionally good care of yourself. My
health habits, by comparison, are horrible, which is another
reason I should have gone first. You were the health nut of the
family. From childhood on, you exercised with more

consistency than anyone I've ever known. You enjoyed physical workouts, enjoyed challenging and pushing yourself. You were always going off to hike or bike or swim.

And you ate so healthfully—always the fresh fruits and innumerable salads without dressing, almost no red meat, low-fat everything. You were a food purist even before your diagnosis, but especially after. You truly believed that diet could have an effect on cancer, prevent a recurrence. You took classes on cancer diets and you stewed those horrible Chinese herbs for teas that you made yourself drink. You were incredibly self-disciplined about what you ate. And for what did you give up all gastronomic pleasures? You died anyway. I'm reminded of that Erma Bombeck quote: "Seize the moment. Remember all those women on the Titanic who waved off the dessert cart."

A year or so before you died, I was listening to a radio talk show hosted by a doctor. The doctor said that a healthful diet might do more harm than good when fighting cancer. His reasoning was based on the fact that cancer cells are voracious; they are the fastest-reproducing cells, along with the cells in hair follicles and the stomach lining. Therefore, the more healthfully you eat, the stronger and healthier you make the cancer cells, thus allowing them to grow even faster than they otherwise would. I was terribly worried when I heard that, because it made sense.

I didn't know whether to mention that theory to you or not. The next time I visited you, I talked to Joe about it and asked him if I should tell you. He said no, that he didn't think anything short of a miracle would make any difference to the outcome in your case. And I hesitated to tell you because you *believed* your cancer diet would help, and attitude was so important in your battle. Should I have told you? Would it have made any difference?

> *Much benevolence of the passive order may be traced to*
> *a disinclination to inflict pain upon oneself.*

~ George Meredith

Dear Sara—

I had an appointment with Dr. Goode this morning. I hadn't been in a month, so I had a lot to go over with her. I described my anguish over Joe's cruelty to you at the very end of your life, the exposure of his true feelings about your marriage, which had to have been devastating to you.

I think it's the first time I've ever seen Dr. Goode shocked, which validated my upset. She even offered an emotional opinion, which is very rare for her. She said, "That's *terrible* behavior, unbelievably cruel. And I suspect that's a factor in why your sister declined and died so quickly, after doing so well for so long." That's what I suspect, too.

I told her of the other things Joe said to me after you died, and of his behavior since—his apparent lack of grief, his immediate talk of dating and remarrying, and his continual dumping on you. Dr. Goode shook her head and said, "It sounds as if he might have a personality disorder." She agreed with me that his attitude and actions will probably come back to bite him.

When I got home, I started researching various mental illnesses and personality disorders. I really want to know what's going on with Joe. I want to understand.

I spent hours searching online, and what I've come up with is Passive-Aggressive Personality Disorder. I've always known that Joe is extremely passive *resistant*; I saw many examples of that when I visited you over the years, and you yourself told me several times that he was the most passive-resistant person you'd ever known. In fact, I've just recalled that another bizarre thing Joe told me just after you died was that he'd never said "No" to you. I remember staring at him and thinking, "Oh yes you did— a thousand times with your passive resistance to everything she ever asked you to do." According to my research, passive resistance is one aspect of Passive Aggressive Personality Disorder. It's an indirect resistance to an authority figure.

Passive-resistant people are afraid to confront the person asking them to do something, so they try to maintain some power and control by procrastinating or "forgetting" or doing an incomplete job or losing things. My God, does that ever describe Joe! I remember your terrible frustration anytime Joe did even a small project around the house—he would either do it at a snail's pace or start to do it at a good pace and then abandon it and leave it unfinished. That's another reason your house is a mess. He refused to hire anyone to do anything, insisting that he could do it himself, and then tortured you with its pace or incompleteness. A coward's way, rather than saying "No."

Passive-Aggressive Personality Disorder can result from relationships that are "covertly hostile but dependent." Well, you were always the primary breadwinner, and often the *only* wage earner, so Joe was financially dependent on you. And since he made no friends of his own over the years of your marriage, he was socially dependent on you as well.

Evidently "perpetual victimhood" is another manifestation of PAPD. Those with the disorder are afraid to confront the person or persons who are the source of their anger and go around feeling "victimized and persecuted." Boy, does that ring true. Joe expresses resentment—now—that everything was done your way: *your* choice of where and how to live, *your* choice of friends. He clearly feels like a victim when, in reality, he didn't make his preferences known or respected. But people with PAPD, I'm learning, accept no accountability, feeling there's nothing they can do to change whatever situation they're in. It seems they don't intentionally act this way; it's unconscious and they don't realize they're doing it. Supposedly, treatment is terribly difficult, since there's no admission or realization that they're acting this way.

The ultimate example of a husband with PAPD is Rip Van Winkle. He would help others (non-authority figures), but neglected his own home and farm and family, in spite of (or because of) his wife's nagging. To escape his wife, he wandered off and supposedly slept for 20 years. He didn't return home until after his wife was dead—i.e., no longer there to make demands of him—and lived happily ever after.

The Rip Van Winkle story is interesting to contemplate just now as I'm trying to analyze Joe, because Joe's primary way of displaying his rebellion against any demands upon him is to go to sleep! During your marriage, if company was due or a household crisis was in progress, he would often suddenly just disappear, without apology or explanation, and could be found asleep in bed. I was there a number of times when he did that, and it was bizarre.

The way to love everything is to realize it might be lost.

~ G.K. Chesterton

Dear Sara—

I've been reading about "anticipatory" grief or "preparatory" grief. That's when someone you love has a terminal illness, and you know ahead of time that he or she is going to die. In the usual course of anticipatory grief, you have a heightened concern for the person when you learn she's terminally ill, and you're depressed at the thought of what she will be going through and how much you'll miss her. You sort of rehearse the death and the aftermath of the death in your mind.

And I did go through that to some extent. But *nothing* prepared me for your actual death. Like you, I was in denial, thinking it wouldn't *really* happen. If anyone in the world could beat this thing, it was you, Sara. You were so strong, so vital, so *alive* that I simply could not in any way, shape or form imagine you dead.

Evidently some people begin detaching from the ill person during anticipatory grief, but it's more common for the relationship and the attachment to intensify during this time. I believe Joe began detaching from you, while the rest of us did the opposite.

Anticipatory grief is not regular grief that just begins earlier. It's not as if grieving ahead of time cuts the grieving on the other side of the death in half. People in general seem to expect you to get over the loss more quickly if the death is one that was expected. But the actual death still comes as a horrible shock, and you begin the grieving process from step one at that point. Anticipatory grief, at least in my case, was kind of a battle between intellect and emotion; my brain knew you were going to die, but my heart could neither believe nor accept it.

Of course the good thing about having forewarning that someone you love is going to die is that you do get a chance to resolve things. You have the opportunity to gradually absorb the reality that you are going to lose the person you love. It's sort of an unreal reality, though. It's natural, I think, to hope for a miracle or a last-minute cure. I still can't believe that the miracle or the last-minute cure never materialized.

I can't help but be grateful for the early warning of your death, because we did get to talk a lot and declare our love for one another. That wouldn't have happened had you died suddenly. Is that selfish of me to be glad for that? Is sudden death better for the one who dies, if harder for those left behind? I just don't know if quicker is better. I can't figure it out. With a slow death, you have the chance to literally and figuratively put your house in order. Is the suffering of a slow death, both physical and psychological, on yourself and on everyone who cares about you worth that advantage?

You told me that there were a few women in your breast cancer support group who didn't want to be tested regularly, who refused to have their tumor marker tests done. They didn't want to know if their cancers had recurred until they had actual symptoms. I know you agonized at first over that same decision of to-know or not-to-know-ahead-of-time, before any symptoms appeared. But when push came to shove, you were someone who *had* to know, and so you had the tests done religiously.

True, it resulted in much more mental anguish for you, because the numbers rose steadily and alarmingly months before any symptoms appeared or tests could confirm that your cancer had returned and where it had metastasized. Despite the added stress, I absolutely believe it was the right decision, Sara. I think you thought so too in the end, because the early warning allowed the doctors to jump right in with treatments that gave you a good extra six months of life. Those six extra months were priceless to you and to us. I'm glad you were brave enough to be tested regularly.

Joe told me that you should have stopped chemo a lot sooner than you did, that the extra time you gained wasn't worth it. Well, it was worth it to *you*. You never considered giving up; to *not* fight was unthinkable to you. You wanted every day and every minute and every second of life you could get. Who can blame you, if that's what you wanted? Battling on despite all odds might not have been everyone's choice, but it was affirmatively yours.

*Nothing fixes a thing so intensely in the memory as the
wish to forget it.*

~ Michel de Montaigne

Dear Sara—

I have to accept that life will never be the same, that *I'll*
never be the same without you. I literally have to learn how to
live my life without you anywhere in it. Even wonderful things
that might happen in the future will be missing some of their joy
because I won't be able to share them with you. And Lisa—her
graduations and marriage and having kids, all will be diminished
because her mom's not here. Others will fill in where they can,
but it won't be the same. Never will she have a special event
that's not ambivalent.

Actually, I shouldn't say that. At some point, when she's
married and has kids, the traditions and memories she'll develop
with her own nuclear family will replace many of those she
associates only with you right now. It might take until she's in
her fifties, but at the point where you might more naturally have
been expected to die—when you would have been in your
80's—she should be able to enjoy holidays and events without
ambivalence. But that's a long way out.

You know what bothers me terribly these days? The word "sister." It hurts to read or hear that word, and it always will. I know it will because the words "mother" and "father" still hurt, all these years after their deaths, especially the cards and advertisements I see and hear everywhere around Mother's Day and Father's Day. To me the word "sister" has but one meaning—you. When I see that word, I have an immediate reaction that feels like a physical blow to my heart, as though someone has punched me in the chest with a clenched fist.

Another thing that bothers me these days is going through catalogs. I get tons of catalogs, and it used to be a pleasure at the end of the day to sit down and go through them all. I always had gifts in mind for you when I did it—birthday or Christmas or "just because" gifts. I knew your tastes as well as I know my own. You were easy to buy for, and you seemed to enjoy my gifts very much. After your diagnosis, I constantly searched for those nightgowns that you liked so well and are hard to find— the short natural cotton ones with flutter sleeves. You were always tremendously pleased and grateful when I'd find one for you. You didn't have time to sit down and search catalogs.

Now when I browse my catalogs, I am overcome with thoughts of you. I see so many things in them that I know you'd love. I pray with the turning of each page that I won't come across a perfect Sara item, because you aren't here to give it to. I especially hurt on those rare evenings when I find one of "your" nightgowns. I think I'll have to give up catalogs for the time being.

One part of my identity that I recognize I'll have to change is my style of dress. I've always imitated your colors, your style. And I'm beginning to realize, lately, that they were *your* colors and *your* style, not the most appropriate or flattering for me. I don't know why I didn't see that before.

I hope it's not the beginning of "separating" from you, Sara, because I don't *want* to separate from you. I think it's just that in looking now at photos and videos of us together, I notice the differences in our size and coloring more than I used to. I don't know if you would have glowed as brightly in any color you chose to wear or if the lovely colors you always wore—the periwinkles and purples and blues and bright whites—contributed to your glow. I wanted to glow like you. I recognize now that your luminescence came from within.

I see now that the colors most flattering to me are the beige and brown tones. They go best with my ashy-silvery hair and subdued complexion and brown eyes. Those are the colors I get the most compliments on when I wear them. In future I'll be buying more of those colors for my wardrobe. In the meantime, I have a closet full of periwinkles and purples and blues and bright-whites, which I'll continue to wear, of course. You and I had a few identical tops that we bought together and wore when we were together, just for kicks. Those, Sara, I don't think I can wear anymore. But I won't get rid of them.

Make no judgements where you have no compassion.

~ Anne McCaffrey

Dear Sara—

Well, now I'm confused. Other than Dr. Goode, there is only one person to whom I've confided any of my real thoughts and feelings about your death and a little of my hurt and anger about Joe's behavior—my friend Lynette. I've been e-mailing her some of my "discoveries" as I research different types of grief and mental illnesses, trying to figure out Joe.

She called last night, and told me off. Or at least that's how I took it. Lynette said that every husband she's ever had (she's had three) could be described or diagnosed as passive resistant. She says it's the nature of the beast. Lynette has met Joe, and although she doesn't like him much said *she* wasn't about to judge him, because she felt that taking care of a terminally ill person is a nightmare for the caretaker and would make anyone act crazy.

Now, I haven't told her everything. I told her about Joe's apparent lack of grief at your death and his immediate search for a new woman, and she knows of your various frustrations with Joe over the years. But I've told only Dr. Goode about what Joe said to you and about you just before and after you died. I don't know why I haven't told anyone else. It somehow seems wrong of me to reveal until I figure it all out.

That aside, could Lynette be right? Am I being too hard on Joe? I know that caretaking a terminally ill person is an awful job, full of physical and emotional stress and strain. Joe took you to all your appointments and tests and chemo sessions. He had to wait on you when you had chemo side effects that put you in bed, which was one or two days every week or two weeks or three weeks depending on your chemo schedule at the time. You napped more and more as time went on, of course, but you were fully functional—showering by yourself, feeding yourself, paying the bills, making phone calls, handling social obligations—literally until the day before you lost consciousness. Actual physical caretaking of you was about as minimal as I've ever heard of with a terminal cancer patient. But who can say what the true psychological toll on Joe was?

You couldn't have had a better attitude; there was no doom and gloom in your house, no self pity on your part at all—or at least none that you revealed. You were cheerful and optimistic all the way. I'm sure that was part of your denial process, but it definitely made it easier on those around you.

Something you once said to me about having cancer made a huge impression. When I visited you about six months before you died, you turned to me one day and said, "I never think about my cancer, never worry about it, never dwell on it. If I did, it would ruin the joy of the day."

I recall staring at you in open-mouthed admiration and more than a little disbelief. How could you *not* think about it? It had recurred, you had liver mets. There was little chance that you were going to beat it. Yet you bounced cheerfully through your days, made plans for the future, never complained. You were an inspiration to others, for sure, but it almost didn't seem human.

I believe that you did put it out of your mind, though. I suspect that was the only way you could get up each morning and accomplish anything, and you did stay amazingly productive to the end.

Proof to me that you truly were optimistic, and not just pretending to be, was that you continued to go to the dentist! Geez, Sara, if I thought there was any chance at all that I might die within the next *year* or two, much less within the next month or two, the last place on earth I'd go would be to the dentist! Yet you kept an appointment to have some fillings re-done a month before you died. You took the bus to the dentist's office and vomited on the bus—you told me that you'd timed it wrong; it was too close to your last chemo. You were so embarrassed. You'd taken the bus because you were wearing morphine patches and hesitated to drive. Joe hadn't wanted to take more time off work to take you to a non-cancer related appointment, and you felt you could handle it alone.

No, knowing all that I do, I don't think I'm being too hard on Joe. I'm appalled by his treatment of you at the end. I'm insulted by his immediate search for a new woman.

Although...maybe I'm "displacing" anger. I read about that just this morning in my study of grief reactions. Maybe I'm furious at you for dying, and I'm turning that rage on Joe. I suppose it's a possibility. I'll have to run that by Dr. Goode the next time I see her. In the meantime I'll continue my focus on Joe, but I promise I'll leave the door open a crack.

Sorry, Lynette—it makes me feel better to try to figure it out, to find plausible reasons for Joe's otherwise inexplicable and very hurtful behavior. Maybe a few years from now I'll have a whole different perspective on Joe. Maybe I'll owe him a huge apology. I have a feeling, however, that this pattern will continue with any future relationships he attempts. With his problems, or what I perceive to be his problems, in order to have a better relationship in the future he should probably find a more traditional, submissive type of woman. But I'll bet you anything he ends up with another strong feminist.

Anne McCurry

*Our ability to delude ourselves may be an important
survival tool.*

~ Jane Wagner

Dear Sara—

Oddly enough, I'm glad you were already unconscious when I got there. We had said our "I love you's," as usual, during our last phone call. Over the preceding year, we had resolved anything and everything that either one of us perceived to be a past hurt or misunderstanding.

If you had regained consciousness after I got there, you'd have *known* you were dying, no doubt remaining. If you had looked at me and said, "Help me, Anne," or, "Please, Anne…don't let this happen," I could not have stood it. I simply could not have borne it, because there was nothing I could do to prevent your death. Somehow, to see that you finally knew you were dying would have been the most heartbreaking thing of all, because you hadn't even begun to make peace with it. I was more than willing to play the denial game with you, since that was the way you wanted to, or needed to, handle death. Maybe it was the way I wanted to, or needed to, handle your death, too.

Which brings me back to Joe. He told you that you were dying while you were still conscious. When you and I last talked on the phone, you said with half-laughing disbelief, "Honestly, they're treating me around here like I'm *dying* or something! I'm not dying!" It was terribly important to you that it not be acknowledged. But Joe himself told me that you had turned to him the day before you lost consciousness and asked, "Do you really think I'm going to die soon?" And he had bluntly answered, "Yes."

What was his motive? More raw cruelty, revenge for a marriage that (in his mind, anyway) had gone bad? Or possibly, more benignly, wanting to give you a chance to make some sort of peace with death while there was still time? I have no idea. I suppose it could have been either or both of those reasons, or even something entirely different..

I do believe, though, that his telling you of his unhappiness with your marriage combined with his telling you straight out that you were indeed about to die hastened your death. But who's to say that wasn't a blessing? It was inevitable, and probably would have occurred within a week or two in any event. Less than two days of unconsciousness, with minimal medical intervention, is definitely a relatively kind death when talking about metastasized breast cancer.

Your journey to that point had not been pain-filled; your doctors, bless them, were wonderful about palliative treatment. You'd been on morphine for months, and the dosage was constantly being fine-tuned to ensure that you were virtually free of pain while still being able to function pretty much normally. So different from when Dad died, remember? It still haunts me that his very last words in life were a plea for medication because he was in so much pain. And his plea was denied. They told him no, he couldn't have any more pain pills, it hadn't been four hours since his last ones. God forbid that this poor, suffering man—who would be dead in a matter of hours—might become addicted to pain pills! Damn them for their hard hearts and compassionless rules. I am so thankful that your doctors were kind and sensible, Sara.

Going fast at the end was probably a good thing. But the *reason* you might have declined and died so very quickly—i.e., Joe's cruel honesty—was definitely *not* a good thing.

Joe told me that your last words to him were, "I don't think I can do this."

Meaning die.

But there wasn't much choice.

I might show facts as plain as day:
But since your eyes are blind, you'd say,
"Where? What?" and turn away.

~ Christina Rossetti

Dear Sara—

Two months today since you died. Sometimes it seems like two hours, at other times years and years.

I was looking at some videos yesterday, taken over the last year of your life. As I watched them, I saw the physical changes in you that I couldn't see very well at the time: the slow weight loss, the gradual bloating around your middle. The worried expression in your eyes, even as your smile remained wide and open and beautiful.

It's funny that I couldn't see that you were physically failing when I was actually with you, but could so clearly see it in the videos. Is it because the camera doesn't lie, while love can? I think being in your physical presence blinded me. The power of your personality and the energy you radiated right up until the end probably distracted me.

Or maybe you instinctively, unconsciously, camouflaged how ill you were. It's a basic survival thing. I know birds do it;

they will act lively and cheerful and energetic, even when very ill. Then suddenly you find them sitting still, all fluffed up. The next thing you know, they're dead. It's natural for them to try their mightiest to appear healthy and active within the flock until they no longer can. If a bird shows signs of illness, it will often be driven out of the flock by the other birds because a sick bird will attract predators, thereby endangering them all.

Technically, the course your disease took was that of "descending plateaus"; you had a long, slow decline over time, with periods of restabilization whenever a new chemo drug kicked in and started working. The doctors came through time after time with something that would stop the cancer in its tracks, for a little while anyway. Finally, though, they ran out of options and ideas; each time a drug stopped being effective, the cancer seemed to come roaring back stronger than before and harder to knock down. They finally suggested that you stop aggressive treatment and concentrate on quality of life and palliative measures for what time remained. You were upset that they were giving up. You weren't ready to. In fact, you never told me that they *had* given up. Joe's the one who told me.

In your last e-mail to me you mentioned that you were having trouble figuring out what day of the week it was, and that people were telling you that you were turning yellow. I'd noticed during our phone calls that week that things were changing; your normally quick and forceful speech had become somewhat hesitant, and your focus seemed to wander from the subject at hand. For the first time, you sounded a little spacey. You mentioned (laughing) that it had taken you an hour to write a check. I was already deeply alarmed about all that, but your e-mail was the first I knew that you were turning yellow.

That news made my heart drop down to the soles of my feet. I knew from asking Dr. Goode about what symptoms to expect that yellowing would signify a dangerous rise in your bilirubin count. She'd told me that counts of 20 to 30 would result in mental confusion and that over 30 meant real brain damage.

And that the end would probably be near at that point. At the time you sent me that last e-mail, your bilirubin count had risen from a single low digit the week before to over 20.

I knew the end could be surprisingly fast, although that wouldn't necessarily be the case. I remembered that Linda McCartney, who also had breast cancer that metastasized to her liver, went amazingly fast at the end. Two days before she died, she was horseback riding and looking great.

As soon as I read your e-mail, I called Joe and asked him when I should come. You didn't want me to come; you knew that my next visit would mean the end was near. That was unspoken but understood between us the last time we parted.

Joe said I should probably come within a few days, and I made reservations as soon as I hung up. I will be forever grateful that I got there in time.

I mentioned before that I thought you looked surprisingly good when I arrived, even though you were unconscious. But Joe took a lot of pictures of you and of us with you during those last two days, and in the photos you *do* look desperately ill, fatally ill. The photos that Joe sent me of those days are awfully hard to look at, but I'm glad I have them. When I study them, I realize that there truly was no hope, no chance that you could have bounced back, if only for a few more days.

At the time, I was a little appalled that Joe was running around taking pictures of you as you lay dying. I don't think you'd have liked that, but I do appreciate having them; they have definitely helped me accept the reality of your death. They are proof positive that you died.

A picture is indeed worth a thousand words, and I think it would take a thousand words to fully describe what I feel as I look at the very last picture ever taken of you. Within a minute or two of your death, Joe took a close-up of your still face framed by that breathtaking sunset. My emotions are in turmoil every time I look at that photo, but I think the main feeling is a heavy, heavy sadness.   Profound sadness.   Sadness that penetrates to the bone.

*We seek to find peace of mind in the word, the formula,
the ritual.
The hope is illusion.*

~ Benjamin Cardozo

Dear Sara—

I got to thinking about the taking of death photos (or mourning photos or corpse photos, as they're also called) after writing to you yesterday, so I did some research. I didn't think it was a common practice, but I wasn't sure why. I guess I thought that most people would find death photos a little morbid. I discovered that people evidently have strong feelings one way or the other on the topic of these photos, either feeling they are disgusting and inappropriate or very important.

Taking death photos used to be commonplace. In many cases, especially in poorer families, the corpse photo was the only photographic image ever taken of the deceased. It was literally the family's only physical memory of the dead loved one, and therefore precious. These days, of course, we have photos of our loved ones spanning their entire lives, so taking one at the time of his or her death doesn't have the importance it once did. Why take a photo of a dead person when we have lots of pictures of them alive and well? It's part of our culture today to disguise and deny death, so why ram it in our faces with a photo of a dead person?

An interesting difference of opinion. I guess the bottom line is that it's a very personal decision, and one that should be respected either way. As I said, I was a little turned off when Joe took all those photos of you in your helplessness and then after you died, but it *has* helped me with the reality of having lost you. I've needed that.

While looking for information on death photos, I found some other stuff I never knew, such as how the custom of flowers at funerals started. In the days before fast transportation (or embalming), the burial of bodies was often delayed while awaiting the arrival of out-of-town relatives or for the photographer to come from a distance to take the death photo. The deceased would start to decompose a little and begin to smell, so flowers were used to mask the odor of decay. That's one custom we still follow, although not for that reason, thank goodness.

Remember I said earlier that I wished we still wore black to demonstrate grief after losing someone? I never knew why black was used for mourning clothing, but I've just read that black was believed to make the mourner inconspicuous so that he or she wouldn't be claimed by Death as its next victim. The reason for a widow wearing black for a year was because it was thought that it would take one full year for the body of her husband to decay in the ground. She was free to re-marry after one year and one day.

There's lots of interesting information about old customs and rituals. They would ring the church bell one time for each year of the deceased person's life. Pregnant women weren't allowed to go to funerals. The eyes of the dead person were closed so that the deceased couldn't appear to be looking at anyone, choosing someone to accompany him or her to the grave. They removed the body feet-first from the home in the belief that if he went head-first, facing back toward the mourners, it might influence another to follow him in death. I don't know whether or not your body was removed feet-first from your house; we were all hiding in Lisa's bedroom when they took you away.

Anne McCurry

*Grief knits two hearts in closer bonds than happiness
ever can; and common sufferings are far stronger links
than common joys.*

~ Alphonse De Lamartine

Dear Sara—

Some days are better than others. Yesterday was bad.
Images of you continually popped up all day long. I associate so
many, many things with you.

There is no way I can think of any aspect of my childhood,
of growing up, without thinking of you. You were there for
everything, front and center. Because we were so close in age,
most activities and milestones were done in tandem—getting our
first bikes, taking ballet and piano and swim lessons, receiving
confirmation in church. You were the maid-of-honor in my
wedding, and I took part in yours. Every growing-up holiday
and vacation was spent together, with our own special family
memories of those events. There's no one to bounce those
memories off now.

Lisa, of course, is in the same boat—more so, in fact. You
two were *so* close. Joe called again this morning, and said Lisa's
having a real bad time. Well, of course she is! He admitted that

he has a hard time empathizing with her, because he just doesn't feel the degree of loss that she does.

The only time I hear real emotion in Joe's voice is when he talks about Lisa. He clearly wants to help her, but doesn't have a clue as to how. He's seen to it that she has both a therapist to talk to and a bereavement group to go to, but it's not the same as if he were able to share the pain with her. He doesn't feel it and can't hide that he doesn't, and that hurts Lisa tremendously. Joe admits that he misses you as Lisa's parent. He acknowledges what a good mother you were, and how much he needs your help with her right now.

But of course if you were here, she wouldn't need help.

Anne McCurry

Sorrow is the great idealizer.

~ James Russell Lowell

Dear Sara—

I came upon something in my grief research that shook me up. It was about idealization of the lost loved one—it can indicate ambivalence or anger or guilt toward the person who died.

That got me thinking about my friend Lynette, whose second marriage was terribly unhappy. She was married to a nasty guy, an emotionally-abusive and selfish man. She often confided to me during that marriage that she was miserable and wanted out. When he died of a sudden heart attack, however, Lynette totally changed her tune. She declared that she had lost her "soul mate," that he was the best husband on earth. She mourned him deeply and apparently sincerely. At the time, I was amazed at her seeming hypocrisy. But now I'm beginning to see that her way of handling her feelings of guilt at being glad she was free of him was to unconsciously idealize him and their marriage. She probably felt she *should* feel some sort of grief, and that was the only way she *could* feel it.

That's 180 degrees different from Joe, who apparently feels no obligation—personal or societal—to feel or show grief, nor does he appear to suffer any guilt for not grieving. Joe has a total inability to pretend, which is why he's an uncomfortable, disconcerting person to be around—you never know what the guy's going to say or do. I don't know if his sort of honesty is admirable or not, but it certainly doesn't ease his way in life.

Getting back to the idealization of a lost loved one, I'm not sure that applies to our relationship because I haven't idealized you just since your death—I idealized *and* idolized you when you were alive, from my earliest memories.

If I scratch my grief just a tiny bit, however, I do indeed find anger just beneath the surface. First of all, I'm angry that a woman as intelligent and health conscious as you could have let this happen. You admitted to me, after your mastectomy, that you'd felt something wrong, something "heavy," in your breast as far back as September. But you had already scheduled your yearly gynecological exam for November, so you made the decision to wait till then to have it checked out.

Maybe it wouldn't have made any difference in the long run, but your tumor turned out to be so large and your type of breast cancer so aggressive that those two months might have made the difference between life and death. Instead of stage three breast cancer, maybe it would have been at stage two or even stage one if you'd gone in immediately. In a way, I can understand your not being too alarmed by the sensation in your breast; after all, there was no history of breast cancer in our family. But you should have run, not walked, to have it checked out. So, yes, I'm mad at you for that.

Okay, if I scratch a little deeper, I'm angry and hurt that you never had enough time for me. You never had enough time for anyone, and we're all a little angry about it. You were too busy—you had so many friends and interests and activities, on top of a time-consuming career, that no one had enough of you. You tried to be there for everyone, even those on the periphery of your life to whom you probably shouldn't have given as much time and attention as you did. As Aesop said, "Please all, and you will please none." We all had just a fraction of your time and attention—even Joe and Lisa, although you did make more time for Lisa than anyone else. But we needed more, and now we'll never have it. Why did you have to keep so damn busy all the time? You wore yourself out. You were stretched way too thin. That had to have impacted your health.

When you were first diagnosed, I remember asking Dr. Goode if there was nothing that could be done to save you, nothing you could do to save yourself? She felt that probably your best chance was to totally change your lifestyle. To be less active and involved with everything and everyone else, and take time to nurture *yourself* for a change, instead of the whole world. I even told you what Dr. Goode said, and you said you'd think about it. But you couldn't do it. You couldn't slow down for a minute. You were greedy for all life and all experiences and all relationships.

Scratch deeper yet and I find the guilt. I know we all drained you. Everyone turned to you for advice and counsel— not just your radio audience, but your multitude of friends and acquaintances and, of course, your family. You felt your role in life was to help others, and you never said "No" to anyone who needed to talk. Your time was necessarily limited with each person, because so many people needed you.

Did we devour you? Did we eat you alive? Did you need to die to get some peace?

How dreadful knowledge of the truth can be when
there's no help in truth!

~ Sophocles

Dear Sara—

I guess I'm not done sounding off, because there are a few more things, and I might as well get them off my chest. One is that if our roles were reversed and I was the one dying, I know you wouldn't have done the things for me that I did for you, because you were too busy. No way would you have flown back to be with me every few months. No way would you have helped me clean my attic or replant my gardens.

I know that, and I also accept it. I used what I had to help you, which was my time and my hands-on work and my love. Your way of supporting me, I think, would have been with *your* strong points—talk and compassion and empathy, as well as practical pointers about treatment options and helpful support groups.

I always hoped I would die first. In fact I fully expected to, just as Mom—the youngest of three sisters—died first. I can't imagine dying without you at my side, gently comforting me at the end. As I said earlier, however, the fact that you will already be there (wherever "there" is) to welcome and guide me when my time comes is oddly comforting. There were lots of places I was scared to go when I was little, but you took me by the hand and led me, lending me your courage. I believe you'll do that when I die.

A question that's recently risen to my consciousness: would you have grieved for me as much as I'm grieving for you, had I been the one to die first? I honestly don't think so. I know you'd have felt terrible and missed me very much, but I don't think you'd have been consumed by grief, as I am for you. You loomed much larger in my life than I ever did in yours, I'm convinced of that. But that's *okay*, Sara, truly, because you never asked me to love you this much. Extreme grief is the price you pay for extreme love, I guess. I don't regret loving you as much as I did, even if I'm paying for it now.

The last, and biggest, thing that's been bothering me: you did something extraordinarily brave about six months before you died. You gave me the story of your life to read, the one that you wrote for Lisa. You asked me to read it even though you knew it might burst my bubble regarding you, might knock you off your pedestal in my eyes. In a way, it did. Certainly, it made you more human and less perfect, which is probably good when all is said and done.

In your story, you admitted that you'd hated me when we were growing up. You felt that our parents had had us too close together, and that you didn't get your fair share of parental attention because I came along too soon after your birth. Because I had some physical problems as a baby and toddler, I got even more attention than would otherwise have been normal. You were jealous, and your sibling rivalry knew no bounds.

You revealed that you deliberately set out to make yourself look like the "good" child and make me seem (and believe I was) the "bad" child. I couldn't believe the things you admitted to doing! For instance, you said Mom and Dad had a list of chores to be done hanging in the kitchen, and that we were to check them off under our names when they were finished. You said that when I'd do a chore, you'd erase my checkmark and check it off under your own name, to make me look bad and you look good! I have no memory of this or the other diabolical things you wrote about. I was so trusting and naïve that I suppose I never looked at the list again once I'd checked off a chore.

Your plot certainly worked; I was the problem child and you were the perfect one, in my mind and everyone else's. You excelled at everything you did, while I did so poorly that I eventually stopped trying to do much of anything. It was terribly hard following you in school. You got straight A-pluses and won every award imaginable. I barely managed C's. So often, I'd have the same teachers you'd had just the year before, and they would expect me to do as well as you. I knew I couldn't no matter how hard I tried, so it seemed pointless to put much effort into it. I slid by.

There is one very cruel incident that I *do* remember, though. It's funny how I'd buried it all these years until I read your book. I was 17, and you sat talking to me one evening, earnestly telling me over and over again that I was simply "not college material" and should give up all thoughts of going to college. I believed you, as I always did, and decided not to even try going. The matter was taken out of my hands, however, when Mom filled out a college application for me and sent it in. They accepted me, and I made Dean's List both semesters I was there. I remember your sending me a postcard at the time that said, "Congratulations, Anne! I knew you could do it! I'm proud of you!" But in your story, you admit that you were dismayed that I'd had some success at college. I guess your dismay didn't last long, since I went only one year to college and then dropped out to marry Tim.

As you know, I was in shock after reading your story. I'd always thought you loved me and wanted what was best for me. I thought the fact that I never amounted to much was due to my own shortcomings, not because of plots against me by the sister I adored!

Well, fortunately, we had time to talk it all out. You cried and asked for forgiveness, which I freely gave, of course. How could I not, at that point? You were dying, and if forgiveness could give you some peace of mind, I gave it with all my heart.

You said you'd suffered tremendous guilt all your adult life over things you'd done to me while we were growing up. You said you'd had years of therapy because of it. In the end, your therapist convinced you to exonerate yourself of all blame because it was not your fault that you were born when you were and I was born when I was and that I had some problems that required extra attention. Well, Sara, it wasn't my fault either! I'm glad you were relieved of all self-blame, but where does that leave *me*?

I'm grateful that you told me everything, because it helps explain a lot about who I am and why I'm the way I am. It was nothing short of courageous of you to make these admissions. When you cried and asked my forgiveness, you said you didn't want to lose me, that you needed me. You recognized that it was a risk, telling me these things.

I appreciate your taking that risk, but I sure wish you'd told me earlier. It could have saved me years of therapy.

The greatest love is a mother's, then a dog's, then a sweetheart's.

~ Polish Proverb

Dear Sara—

Oh, God…another call from Joe. You won't believe what he said this time. He wants to get rid of Roscoe. He started by asking me how long dogs live. I told him 12 years or more, with good care and good luck. Roscoe's only five. There was a brief silence, then he said that Roscoe was your dog, and he'd never liked him. He hinted that he would be asking me to take him at some point in the not-too-distant future.

Of course I'll take Roscoe. I love all dogs, and I especially love Roscoe because you loved him. He's a handsome boy, and good-natured and smart as anything. Although he's been pretty subdued since you died, according to Joe. "Pining" is how he put it. I know the feeling.

But what about Lisa? She loves Roscoe too, although she always recognized that he was more your dog than anyone else's. I expect Roscoe has turned, or will turn, to Lisa more and more now that you're gone. He's another tie to you, an important one, so I can't believe she'd want to see him go. I'll

81

have to call and talk to Lisa about it, but I don't know if Joe has even run this by her yet. I don't want this new bit of betrayal to come from me first.

Joe's excuse for getting rid of him is that Lisa will probably be going off to college next year, and it will be just he and Roscoe, all alone, and he doesn't like him and doesn't want him around. I'm not so sure Lisa *will* be going off to college next year, though. I don't know if she'll be ready to take that on by then. She's emotionally much younger than her years, and now she's had this horrible blow of losing you, the main support person in her life. She was only 14 when you were first diagnosed, and she seems to have stuck there. I don't know what she'll do if she doesn't go off to college. I can't see her wanting to stay in your house if Joe has another woman by then. Yet the first year of college is such a rough adjustment, emotionally and academically and socially.

Rest assured, Sara, I'll be glad to take Roscoe if it's okay with Lisa. You wouldn't want him living in a house where he's disliked and unappreciated. He'll be loved and taken good care of here with me.

There is no wealth but life.

~ John Ruskin

Dear Sara—

Yesterday was rough. I thought about you all day and most of the night. Maybe it was the Joe/Roscoe thing that set me off, but I kept thinking about things that will never be.

You were amazing—you made plans for the future right up to the end, as though you still had years ahead of you. But you also went out and bought your cemetery plot. What an *agonizingly* ambivalent way to have to live. I don't know how you did it. You must have hoped against hope and waited for the miracle that never came. I did, too.

You'll never be a grandma, and you wanted with all your heart to be one. Our mother and our grandmothers on both sides didn't live long enough to be grandmas either, and you so much wanted to break that miserable pattern.

And you'll never get to have the kind of house you wanted. The last time we went shopping together, two months before you died, you said that if you ever moved to a new house or got to totally redecorate the one you were in, you wanted to do it entirely in a Southwestern theme. You had been saying that for

83

years. I didn't say anything, of course, but my heart was breaking because I was pretty sure you wouldn't live to get the chance to do it. Your house is an eclectic mix of antiques you bought at yard sales, some inherited oriental stuff and a few newish J.C. Penney pieces. You longed to have an attractive, pulled-together theme. We did the best we could in the short time we had with your living room last year, and it turned out nicely, I thought. It was clearly only a temporary re-do in your mind, though.

Something else that bothers me is that I didn't buy you that Pashmina shawl you admired. When we shopped together about a year ago, you flung a gorgeous periwinkle blue Pashmina shawl around your shoulders. It was made for you; you looked beautiful in it. It was terribly expensive, so you didn't even consider buying it. Why didn't I buy it for you? You would have had months of enjoyment with it. I just cheapened up, I guess. I'd come laden with gifts for you and had already way overspent, but what would it have mattered in the end? I'm sorry I didn't buy it for you, Sara.

I know the only gift of value to you would have been longer life. Since I couldn't give you that, I wish I'd gotten you everything that you'd ever wanted of earthly possessions.

*The foolish man seeks happiness in the distance, the wise
grows it under his feet.*

~ J. Robert Oppenheimer

Dear Sara—

Are you ready for this? I had an e-mail from Janis this
morning, who'd had an e-mail from Joe. Joe is interested in a
particular woman, and has been since several months before you
died. Whoever he was after, however, has turned him down
flat—and now he's trying Internet dating!

What is his goddamned *hurry*, anyway? And to try to find a
mate online—my God, talk about asking for trouble. What kind
of wife for himself and stepmother to Lisa will he find through
an Internet dating service? I didn't think he could do anything
more to shock me, but he's managed to. If anyone should take
his time and try to get his head on straight before making any
life-changing decisions, it's Joe.

It's sad that Joe didn't, or couldn't, appreciate what he had in
you. You put up with his myriad of personal oddities, and you
were invariably supportive of him. You defended Joe, never
letting anyone put him down in your hearing, even though he
often made you crazy. I'm betting that his next relationship

won't last long. Who could have the patience with him that you did?

I'll try and find out who the woman was who told him to get lost. I feel like sending her a bouquet of flowers for having such good sense. Although maybe it was common decency, because what kind of woman would start dating a man who's just lost his wife? Especially one who does nothing but badmouth the late wife? It seems to me that would be a huge red flag.

*By the time the fool has learned the game, the players
have dispersed.*

~ Ghanaian Proverb

Dear Sara—

I found out who the woman is. Her name is Catherine, and he met her in one of his innumerable support groups, about six months before you died. I have no idea what she's like or how old she is or what she looks like. Her husband was terminally ill with cancer when he met her, and has since died.

How ironic, because it was you who pushed Joe to get involved with all those support groups. You worried that he might need emotional support in dealing with your illness as it progressed and, if the worst happened, your death. Right.

Learning about Catherine explains a *lot*, and I'm grateful to begin to solve the mystery of why he seemed to have changed so much during your last few months. I can see now why he seemed impatient for your death; he'd found a new honey—or thought he had—and was eager to get on with it. I don't know if it was all a fantasy in his head, or if this Catherine was responsive at some point or not. She undoubtedly was vulnerable, with her husband's illness and recent death. If her marriage was at all happy and she's mourning her husband, she must be repulsed by Joe's behavior. On the other hand, if her marriage was ambivalent, like Joe's, then maybe they both thought for a while that they were soul mates. All I know is that she's told him to go away and stop bothering her.

I've kept my Tim abreast of everything right along. He knew about my alarm at Joe's attitude the last few months of your life, and he knows how upset I've been about how Joe's acted since your death. Tim never liked Joe, just never could stand the guy. I've got to tell you he was a little suspicious of you for years, too, Sara; being a rather conservative male, he was somewhat uncomfortable around a feminist. But after the first few years, he liked you a lot. He came to admire your strength and intelligence and, especially, your spirit and courage in fighting your cancer. Also, he saw that you were a good and loyal sister to me, and recognized how important our relationship was. He cried with true regret when you died.

Tim saw that your marriage was not a typical one, at least by his standards. He knows, as I do, that you couldn't have married or stayed married to a strong man. Last night when I was talking to him about the differences between Joe and you that led to conflicts in your marriage, Tim's comment was, "Sara wanted a puppy dog for a husband, and she got one. But he pissed all over her rug." Although a little crudely put, he's right. That pissing on the rug is a perfect analogy for Joe's passive resistance, which frustrated you so.

*Not to have control over the senses is like sailing in a
rudderless ship, bound to break to pieces on coming in
contact with the very first rock.*

~ Mahatma Gandhi

Dear Sara—

Janis called last night, and we had a good talk. She was a
wonderful friend to you, and I feel as if she's my friend too now.
I feel more connected to you when I talk with her. I guess I
don't have to tell you that she misses you terribly.

Oddly enough, Joe's evidently been going around telling
everyone what he's up to—the pursuit of Catherine, the Internet
search for a woman. All have noted his lack of grief and his
seeming happiness at being "free" and the negative things he
says about you. They are shocked and angry. Janis says it's
terribly upsetting for her and other of your friends to be with
him, but they're hanging in there because of Lisa. Janis assured
me that Lisa *is* aware that Joe's behavior is not that of a normal
grieving spouse, that Lisa realizes something is very wrong. I
was tremendously relieved to hear that.

Janis thinks Joe's got a fantasy life going on in his head—
freedom, a new woman, a new life, happy ever after. She told

me that Joe admitted to her that his support groups are worried about him and have suggested that he might be suffering from Post Traumatic Stress Disorder. I'll do some research on that.

In spite of how Joe's acting now, Janis believes that he truly did love you. Well, I had thought so too until the last couple of months of your life. She's also a little critical of you, Sara, in that you didn't help Joe prepare for your death. She feels that he couldn't deal with it by himself. Maybe that's when he started escaping to his fantasy life.

Actually, it's true that you didn't help any of us ahead of time to deal with your death. You did encourage Joe to go to support groups in case the worst happened (and look what that led to), and you did write your book for Lisa. Other than that, nothing. You didn't say goodbye to any of us. Asking me the last time we parted if everything was resolved between us was by far the closest you came to saying goodbye to anyone. Accepting the inevitable and talking about it probably would have helped all of us, Sara. Even you.

Although Janis can't stand Joe right now, she's dredging up much more compassion for him than I've been able to. Even though he's being so obnoxious, she feels he's terrified and confused, deep down, and doesn't consciously realize it. She thinks he's totally lost his moorings and is adrift. It makes a certain amount of sense, since he was dependent on you for all major decisions, all social interactions, etc. Janis says she and your other friends are convinced Joe's heading for a crash at some point.

*Anger and intolerance are the twin enemies of correct
understanding.*

~ Mahatma Gandhi

Dear Sara—

Nope, it's not Post-Traumatic Stress Disorder. I checked it out, and it just doesn't fit. PTSD results from major, usually sudden, catastrophic events—rapes, plane crashes, kidnappings, earthquakes, etc. It can also result from an ongoing traumatic experience, such as being a POW. It doesn't seem to be associated with the normal bad things that happen in life, though, no matter how painful. The loss of a spouse after a long illness just doesn't fit the criterion.

So I'll stick with my own amateur diagnosis of Joe: absent grief when you died, resulting from the Passive-Aggressive Personality Disorder that caused his ambivalent feelings toward you. It fits, and it feels right. I don't ordinarily feel all that comfortable with labels, but when you're totally in the dark about why someone's acting the way he is, it's tremendously helpful to search until you find some explanation that seems to fit the behavior. Otherwise it would be confusing and hurtful ad infinitum. Not that it's not still hurtful, because it is, but at least I think I know where he's coming from now.

I had an appointment with Dr. Goode yesterday, and I asked her if there was a possibility that my anger toward Joe might be displaced anger. Meaning that I might be so mad at you for dying—or just plain mad that you *did* die—that I have to find a target for that rage. She said that was a very good insight, and that it's possible that's where some of my anger toward Joe is coming from, although she agrees that his actions are legitimate cause for me to be hurt and angry.

Evidently it's not all that uncommon to have displaced anger when someone you love dies. Not only is the person no longer here to be mad at, but it feels wrong to feel anger toward someone who's died. So you get mad at the doctors or at God or some other target. In this case, Joe made it easy to direct my anger toward him. So I'll have to add some displaced anger on my part to the blend as I try to sort things out.

The friends who listen to us are the ones we move toward, and we want to sit in their radius.

~ Karl A. Menninger

Dear Sara—

I had an e-mail from a friend this morning, and it bothered me. She's someone that I had considered a good friend, but she sure hasn't been there for me since you died. Now that I think back, she wasn't there long before you died either. She keeps asking why I'm not communicating more with her, but I feel we don't have much in common right now. My e-mails to her speak of the pain of losing you and adjusting to life without my sister, while her e-mails back to me ignore what I've written and invariably deal with what she's making for dinner that night, what decorating she's doing in her house…nothing of substance. She totally ignores my pain and my need to talk about you.

I have a couple of other friends who also seem to want to sweep what I'm going through under the rug. If they ask me how I'm doing and I begin to respond honestly, they'll interrupt and brush aside what I've just said. They've both said things like, "Well, let's not talk about that sad subject. Let's enjoy the evening." Then they go on to chat about "cheerful" things, while

I stand there surprised and confused, feeling as if I've somehow committed a faux pas by mentioning my pain.

I don't know why some people react like that. Are they shallow? I would not have thought so of these particular people. Is it fear? Possibly, maybe even probably. Whatever it is, they're clearly uncomfortable with the subject of death.

Changing the subject, trying to distract someone from mourning...that's not helpful. I think many people who've just suffered a loss *need* to talk. I believe the mourner should be allowed, even encouraged, to talk all they want to or need to, if they so desire. The best thing a friend or acquaintance can do is listen, whether they're comfortable or not. They don't have to say a word; just *listen*.

There are, I realize, some mourners who *don't* want to talk about their losses, and that's fine too. The best advice I could give anyone is to follow the mourner's lead—if she wants to talk, let her; if she doesn't want to bring the subject up, then go along with that.

It's funny, but how people act at the time someone you love dies is never forgotten. I can remember Dad, 40 years after his mother's death, describing with hurt and more than a little anger how a cousin made a fuss about riding in the hearse on the way to the cemetery. I remember everything especially nice or anything inappropriate or upsetting that was said or done at Mom's and Dad's funerals and, of course, at the time of yours, Sara. Memories of things that happen at highly emotional times tend to be indelible memories.

Sympathy cards are extremely important. They mean a lot. It's *so* important to send a sympathy card, and just as important to write a note on it. If nothing personal is written on the card, it seems like sending the card was an etiquette thing, a polite duty, rather than anything you have any sincere feeling about. But even a message-less card is preferable to no card. You'll never be forgiven if the friend who lost a loved one doesn't hear from you, receives no acknowledgment at all from you at this time of all times. Not knowing what to say is not an excuse; you *have* to say or do something.

I got a lot of sympathy cards when you died, Sara. Some of them had messages I'll cherish forever, and I'll always have a special place in my heart for those who sent them. But there were a couple of people I fully expected to hear from, and did not. Quite honestly, it's difficult for me to consider them friends any longer. Sorry, Sara—I'm just not as tolerant and nonjudgmental as you.

What we do for ourselves dies with us. What we do for others and the world remains and is immortal.

~ Albert Pine

Dear Sara—

Last night was different; I had a full night of sound sleep—a rare event since your death—and had lots of dreams. One particularly vivid dream was about you. A group of us were at your home, although your house in the dream was very different from your real-life home—it was some kind of cedar A-frame or chateau, very spacious and bright with soaring ceilings. We had gathered to wait for you to die. But then you suddenly went away—you had decided to go visit Mom and Dad for a week even though, in reality, they'd been dead for more than 20 years at the time you did die. You were carried off on a stretcher to visit them. You were naked and one-breasted in all the scenes of this dream.

We all just sort of milled around during the week you were gone, waiting for you to return so we could get on with it. Joe hung in there with us until the day before you returned, and then he couldn't stand it any longer and he left. He wanted to get on with his life. He moved out of your house and in with his girlfriend—who turned out to be Barbara Striesand!

You returned home on a stretcher. We dreaded having to tell you that your husband had left, but we had to. You looked dismayed but also accepting. You were sad and hurt that Joe couldn't wait till you died to start a new life, but you told us you understood the strain he'd been under and didn't blame him. That's all I remember of the dream.

Sara, you were a remarkably understanding and compassionate person in life. You accepted all sorts of bad behavior from the people around you by finding reasons for their behavior that would allow you to understand and excuse it. Was the dream last night a message from you for me to forgive Joe? I have a strong suspicion that it's been you who has led me to search for reasons for Joe's behavior. My usual reaction to events is to respond from pure emotion; this slow and careful search for answers has been quite a departure from the norm for me. It's more the way you would have responded, which is why I suspect you might be guiding me.

I'm trying, Sara.

Bereavement is a darkness impenetrable to the
imagination of the unbereaved.

~ Iris Murdoch

Dear Sara—

I obsessed about you all night long. I didn't fall asleep till
5:30 this morning, and I've been dragging around all day. I
haven't even gotten dressed. The weather's been gray and cold
and dreary day after day for so long. That probably adds to my
depression, but it also seems appropriate for the grieving process
I'm locked into. The rare sunny days are almost an unwelcome
intrusion.

This isn't the first day that I haven't gotten dressed. There
have been a lot of days that I haven't found the energy or
enthusiasm to get dressed and put on a little makeup and face the
day. I let my hair go too long between washings, and it's been at
least six months since I had it cut. I've gained weight. Crying is
an almost constant state with me these days. I wonder if anyone
has ever ended up with a salt depletion from crying too much?

This all started before you died, although it's definitely
worsened since. But it's all grief-related. Do you realize that in
the 18 months before your death, I lost five of my babies? My

21-year-old cat, my 15-year-old dog, my ancient mare and gelding and, in some ways worst of all, my one-year-old cat. All except the last had had long, wonderful lives; even so, each one of their deaths was devastating. I hadn't lost an animal in years and years until that unbelievable string of losses occurred.

All during that 18-month period, the biggest loss of all— you—loomed. I thought I'd lose my mind. Loss piggybacked upon loss; I couldn't begin to recover from one death before another occurred. There were days when I wanted to stay in bed and pull the covers up over my head and scream, "No more!" How could I possibly handle more?

But then, of course, there *was* more—you died.

These days I feel like a walking soap opera. I feel as if people don't want to be around me because I might depress them, or they might think that bad things happening are contagious and will rub off on them. I feel like grief incarnate.

I also feel a little selfish at being so totally self-absorbed with my losses. I remind myself to look at what others have lost, both throughout history and in the present day—millions of Jews during the Holocaust, thousands of people at a time in a single earthquake.... Whole families wiped out together for no reason other than the sick bigotry of a madman or a sudden act of Nature. At least something concrete and semi-understandable killed you: a disease. That should make your death easier to accept than a death that is totally nonsensical, but somehow it doesn't. A rose by any other name is still a rose, and a death by any other name—genocide, accident, nature, cancer—is still a death. It just plain *hurts*.

When one after another of my animals died so close together, I couldn't understand what was going on. It seemed way beyond coincidence. It finally dawned on me that there might be a message here, that maybe God was toughening me up to prepare me for the unimaginable pain of losing you. That's the only thing that made any sense to me. Was I right?

I remember what you said on that one rare occasion when you admitted to me that at times you struggled to understand why you had been stricken with terminal breast cancer in your prime. With a philosophical shrug you said, "In time, all will be revealed." You said you felt there was some reason this had come to you, that it wasn't simply random bad luck. I think it would be helpful for anyone to think that, rather than that it was just an unlucky roll of Fate's dice, having no real purpose or meaning. It is my fervent hope that all *has* been revealed to you now, Sara, and that the reason was a damn good one.

*The surest way to corrupt a youth is to instruct him to
hold in higher esteem those who think alike than those
who think differently.*

~ Friedrich Nietzsche

Dear Sara—

Here's something that happened that I never told you about.
My friend Lynette has a son, Jason, who is a remarkable kid,
extraordinarily sensitive and empathetic for a teen-ager. I've
known him all his life, and we're close. He stopped by to say
hello one day about a year before you died. I'd just heard from
you that your cancer had metastasized to your liver, and I knew
what that meant. I must have shown my distress, although I
remember consciously trying not to.

When Jason walked in, he grinned at me and said, "How are
you?" He's a polite kid, so I assumed it was just the usual
mouthing of a commonly-asked question and automatically
responded, "Fine, thanks." After all, how many people really
want to know when they ask how you are? Jason paused,
though, and touched my arm. He looked into my eyes and said,
"No, how are you *really?* I can tell something's wrong."

Well, that opened the floodgates. I started crying and found myself telling him all about your situation. We talked for an hour, and Jason offered some amazing insights for one so young. He said, "I think I'd rather die when I'm middle-aged than when I'm old. It might be better to die then, rather than live to be old and lonely and ignored. You know, if you're old all your accomplishments would be behind you, and nobody would remember what you were and what you did when you were younger. Maybe it's better to go out when you're on top."

Of course, that perspective is from someone who probably sees middle age as being a thousand years away, and he'll most likely think very differently as he approaches that time of life. Still, the more I thought about it, the more good points I found with his comment. Let's face it, there *is* much more tragedy and heartbreak involved when someone dies at a younger age than when someone lives to a ripe old age and then dies. In fact, the amount of grief and heartbreak often seem directly proportionate to the age of the deceased; more for younger, less for older.

The elderly often outlive their friends and family, and all too frequently there isn't the loving care and concern during their final days that a younger person receives. You, Sara, were surrounded by those who loved you in your last days, and who did everything we could to make you more comfortable and ease you on your way. Had you died in your 80's, would anyone have been around to care and to help? Impossible to know.

You died while at the top of your career, and that's how people will remember you. Do you remember that when Mom had to be moved into the nursing home, we took in a newspaper article written about her in her prime? We framed it and hung it on the wall near the head of her bed, so that the staff would realize she had been a real person, a woman with an interesting life and career, not just that empty shell in the bed. At least Lisa will never have to do that for you.

The next thing Jason said that day was that if you didn't die now maybe something horrible would happen in your life, something too painful to bear, and your early death will have spared you that. Such a thought had never occurred to me, and it made more than a little sense, particularly paired with your "In time, all will be revealed" comment. If Joe were going to be killed in a pileup or, God forbid, some horrible illness or event were to happen to Lisa, that would be worse than death for you. I absolutely believe that.

Also, I know for a fact that what you feared above all else in life was that you would get early-onset Alzheimer's disease, as Mom did. Dad, of course, died of cancer. Having watched both parents suffer, you and I agreed that if we had to choose between Alzheimer's or cancer as a way to decline and die, we'd choose cancer. Maybe your death from cancer spared you Mom's fate. Alzheimer's is worse than death.

Bless Jason. He brought a new way of looking at things to the table.

The next time I saw Dr. Goode after talking to Jason, I asked her if I should tell you what he said. I wasn't at all sure that I should; I didn't want to offer a possible reason for why this was happening to you that would freak you out. I was afraid it would up your anxiety level 100 per cent to think you might possibly be dying in order to spare you the agony of Lisa being raped or murdered or something! On the other hand, if cancer was possibly going to spare you from Alzheimer's, you'd have appreciated that theory.

Dr. Goode agreed that I should not tell you at that time, and play it by ear toward the end, depending on your needs then. But because you were unconscious when I got there, the dilemma never presented itself.

For all I know, though, you'd already thought of these possibilities. You always were miles ahead of everyone else.

There is no greater grief than to remember days of joy when misery is at hand.

~ Dante

Dear Sara—

Three months today since you died. I know the first year is the hardest, so I guess I can consider myself one quarter through the worst of this pain. I'm exhausted—grieving is hard, hard work. But I know that the only way to get through it is to get through it.

I know ahead of time that your birthday will be the hardest day of all to get through, with the day that is the one-year anniversary of your death running a close second. Those days are so universally painful that they have a term applied to them: "anniversary grief." It's not just those days, though; the first *everything* after you lose someone you love is like ripping open the thin, fragile scab that has begun to form over the wound. I know I'll have to struggle through one complete year, through each changing season and past all holidays and dates I especially associate with you, before this grief will begin to lose some of its raw power.

Our parents made big deals of our birthdays, remember? They'd take us out to dinner at the restaurant of our choice. Mom, who didn't really know how to cook, would get us each a fancy bakery birthday cake with our names and ages on them. They didn't taste like anything, but they were pretty.

Sometimes we had separate parties and sometimes they were combined, since our birthdays were only a month apart. You hated the combined parties, because you wanted your own special day, not diluted by having to share with me. I wonder, from my perspective now, if Mom and Dad combined the parties to make it more festive for me, because you had many friends to invite to your parties and I had few to invite to mine. The differences in popularity were less obvious if there was one party for both of us. I can hear you hooting at the idea, and I admit it's a stretch to believe they had enough sensitivity and insight to do that, but I suppose it's remotely possible.

I can't imagine wanting to celebrate my own birthday this year. Memories of my childhood birthdays are indelibly intertwined with yours, and I've never in my adult life had a birthday without a call and card and present from you. Those were the highlights of the day. No, I'd just as soon ignore my birthday this time around.

Our birthdays were very special to our parents and to each other. Happy days. And now, because they *were* such special and happy days, the total reverse will be true: specially unhappy days.

Anne McCurry

> *There are two worlds: The world we can measure with*
> *line and rule, and the world that we feel with our hearts*
> *and imagination.*

~ Leigh Hunt

Dear Sara—

Sometime during your last six months, you briefly abandoned your cheerful facade and told me that if people wanted to know exactly how you felt and what you were going through, they should read *Seeing the Crab: A Memoir of Dying Before I Do* by Christina Middlebrook (Basic, 1996). I immediately bought the book and read it straight through. But there was nothing in there I didn't already know, Sara. I'm your *sister*; words never had to be spoken between us for me to know how you suffered, physically or mentally.

I believe I know how you felt with all the ups and downs of your cancer: the shock and disbelief of the original diagnosis; the pure fear when hearing the death-sentence first path reports; the determination to fight this disease and not let it control or deter you; the roller coaster of emotions depending on whether your tumor marker numbers were up or down; the bleak dismay and feeling of helplessness when the proof was in that the cancer had recurred and metastasized; and the mind-wrenching ambivalence about whether you should make plans to live or to die.

I believe I know how you felt at each chemo treatment—the dread before, the stoicism during, the sickness and exhaustion after. I imagined the pain and discomfort of all the side affects, which varied with each new type of chemo: nausea, baldness, neuropathy, the cracked-open skin on your feet, mouth sores, loss of appetite, constipation, fatigue. I felt them all with you, often with my body as well as my spirit. Didn't you know that, Sara? You were my heart walking around outside my body.

Remember when I visited you during the original round of treatments three years ago? You were in bad shape because you'd chosen the most aggressive treatment possible. You said to me at that time that if that rough protocol gave you two or three good years, it would all be worth it. But you didn't get anywhere near that amount of good time. It was less than a year after you finished your initial round of treatments—surgeries, chemo and radiation—that your numbers started going up, although it took months more for the doctors to figure out where the cancer had recurred.

Two or three good years didn't seem like too much to ask. You loved life, and had everything to live for. You had taken good care of yourself your entire life. You felt betrayed by a body that was stubbornly harboring and nourishing an insidious disease, a killer foe. Always before in control of your life, you were helpless to stop this. Everyone was.

Anne McCurry

*The world is a book, and those who do not travel, read
only a page.*

~ Saint Augustine

Dear Sara—

Earlier I spouted off about some nasty things I found out
you'd done to me when we were growing up and how they'd
affected me lifelong. Well, turnabout is fair play, so I have to
mention the many good things you brought to my life.

Travel, for instance. I hate to travel, as you well know, and I
would probably never have journeyed anywhere if it weren't for
you nudging me. It wasn't just that I had to pack a suitcase and
get on a plane and fly across the country if I wanted to see you,
although that was a huge incentive. It was also the various side
trips you insisted we take when I visited you. I know you felt I
was a little too insulated in the layers of my quiet life, and you
wanted me to have memorable experiences every time we got
together. When I think of all the places I would never have gone
and all the things I wouldn't have done if it weren't for you, I'm
more grateful than I can say.

You enriched my life in many, many ways—from the
wonderful women authors you introduced me to and got me

reading, to exciting restaurants that were my first experiences with ethnic foods and good coffees. Your lifestyle and friends were 180 degrees different than mine, and it was an education to visit you and get together with your friends. I grew intellectually, emotionally and politically because of you.

I think the greatest gift you gave me, though, was laughter. Laughter was a priority in your life. I'll especially miss your sense of humor. When we'd get together, I'd find myself laughing until my stomach hurt, and that was different and good for me, the serious one. You were so much fun.

Sometimes it was the things you said, but just as often it was the clumsy things you did. I've never seen such a klutz! Your clumsiness (and your ability to laugh at it) is what saved you from being a bit intimidating, I think; it made you entirely human and lovable and offset what might otherwise have been your somewhat daunting intelligence and accomplishments. People found themselves thoroughly comfortable when meeting you for the first time—you were so natural and down-to-earth, friendly and funny and empathetic. You inspired instant friendship in others, and your circle of friends grew to gargantuan proportions throughout your lifetime.

From our first official visit as adults to our last visit two months before you died, you had me in stitches with your clumsiness. On that first visit, Tim and I had recently married and moved into our own place, remember? Everything was brand spanking new—the building itself, the one-bedroom apartment and every single one of our possessions. I was very proud of it all. You were still in college, and when you came home for summer break I invited you over for dinner. It was the first meal I'd ever made for company. I didn't know the first thing about cooking, of course (having been raised by a non-cooking mother), but I managed to come up with something edible.

I gave you a tour of our immaculate little place and then started dinner. I'd left the utensil drawer partially open as I worked, and the first thing you did was to open a bottle of soda, set it on the counter above that drawer and then accidentally knock it over. Sticky soda flooded my shiny new silverware, all the drawers beneath it and the floor below. What a mess! I was a little nervous every time you visited after that, thinking you would spill or break something. And you never let me down—you did every time! In fact, one word that I will forever associate with you is "OOPS!"

The last time we were together at your place, we went out the back door to get in your car, and you detoured to toss a piece of trash in the garbage. But instead of tossing the trash, which was in your left hand, you tossed your keys, which were in your right hand. They plummeted straight down through three feet of stinky garbage to the bottom of the can, and you and I—all dressed up to go out to lunch—fished frantically through the filth to find them, laughing hysterically. It was just so typical.

Sara, I owe you a lot. You invested too much time and energy in mobilizing me to let it wither away. I know you wouldn't want me to stagnate at this point, with you not here to prod me. Once I get past the worst of this mourning, I promise I'll start living again.

Beauty is the purgation of superfluities.

~ Michelangelo

Dear Sara—

Here's something else I never told you: the reason I let my hair grow long. I know you wondered about it. My reason for letting it grow is simple—if and when I'm diagnosed with cancer and have to undergo chemo, I'll be able to cover my baldness with a wig made from my own hair.

I believe my turn will come, unless something else gets me first. *So* many people in our family have died of cancer although, strangely, no two have been felled by the same type of cancer. There seems to be a horrible susceptibility to cancers is in our genes. I feel as though I have "Doomed" stamped on my forehead.

Your wig was very nice; it was expensive and well made. But it wasn't you. Nothing could be just like your own sparkling silver hair with its thick, springy texture, the cowlick on the crown of your head, and that one little dark gray spot at the nape of your neck.

How you hated your wig! You found it hot and uncomfortable and despised the phoniness of it, even though it didn't look the least bit phony. You often chose to go bald instead of wearing it, and people's reactions be damned. You told me that when you'd go out without your wig, everyone complimented you on how good you looked, telling you that you had an unusually nicely-shaped head. I was prepared to not be upset, therefore, when I first flew out to visit you after you lost your hair. But I was stunned when I saw you without your wig. You looked like an alien! It scared me to death. You were still beautiful, don't get me wrong; your beauty went way beyond hair. But it was just such a shock.

It was after that trip that I decided to let my hair grow. If and when I get cancer and lose mine to chemo side effects, I won't go around without my wig. It should be hard to tell that it *is* a wig, since it will be made of my own hair. Vanity? Sure. I don't have your courage, Sara.

I found out that hair has to be at least ten inches long, and preferably 12 inches, in order to have a wig made from it. It can't have any chemical damage, which is another reason I'm glad I stopped coloring my hair. It's thick and healthy and all natural, at this point. I've surpassed the minimum length now; my hair is 14 inches long. I'll have a couple of inches trimmed soon, because it's getting awfully unwieldy to work with.

Write injuries in sand, kindnesses in marble.

~ French Proverb

Dear Sara—

Joe called again yesterday. For the very first time, he asked how *I'm* doing with my grief. That was different, and very much appreciated. Joe, of all people, knew how close you and I were. But I've noticed that even when the bond with a sister or brother is extremely close, the ones who get the bulk of the concern after the sib dies are the spouse and children (and the parents, if still living), not the sibling. I don't know what Joe's been ruminating about that made him suddenly ask how I'm doing with all this, but I'm glad he did.

He's been dating a lot and has found someone "very special." He actually told me that. He admitted that Lisa is having a terrifically hard time with this development. Joe knows she is and is sorry about it, but is nonetheless plowing ahead with the relationship. He's not hiding it from her at all, even though he must realize that it would be both smarter and kinder to do so.

I can't understand it. I thought that above all else Joe was a good father and would always put Lisa's well being before his

113

own, particularly when she's in such a fragile emotional state from having recently lost her mom. I fear for Lisa. She must feel totally abandoned. It must seem as if she's lost a dad as well as a mom. It's too much.

Lisa's not reaching out to anyone now—not to me or to other relatives or to your friends or even her own. We all want to help, but she won't let us. She's totally withdrawn, and I'm guessing she's deeply depressed. I e-mail her often, but she doesn't respond. I'm not sure she even reads my e-mails. She won't take calls from anyone. I'm praying that her therapist is an excellent one; she badly needs a safe place and someone to talk to who has the wisdom to help her at this time.

Lisa's at an especially difficult age to have lost her mother, I think; mature enough to realize the enormity and all the ramifications of losing you, while at the same time not mature enough or experienced enough to handle it. It's extremely unfortunate that the very first loss she's experienced in life has been the loss of her mother. If she'd already lost a grandparent or a cousin or even a family pet before this, she'd have had at least a nodding acquaintance with grief before losing someone so major in her life.

If only Joe could have at least *pretended* to grieve for you and if only he could have waited a decent interval before beginning to date…. If he could have done those things, Lisa would not be in the trouble she's in now, in my opinion. I never before realized what a handicap an inability to pretend is, and how destructive it can be. You would be heart broken at how your little family has fallen apart so completely since your death, Sara.

I need to make a list of Joe's good and bad points at this time in order to see him more clearly and try to be as fair as I can be at the end of all this research and thought.

Joe's good points: until now, he's been a wonderful father to Lisa, fully as committed and involved as you in her upbringing. He took good physical care of you during your illness. He stayed with you all those years, through good times and bad. He saw that I got out to you in time to be with you when you died. He has all sorts of talents and capabilities, even if he's never used them very productively. He's highly intelligent. He stays in regular touch with me and keeps me informed, from his unique perspective, about how Lisa's doing.

Joe's bad points: his maddening passive-resistant behavior, which often made your life miserable. His unwillingness to get a steady job, thereby putting enormous pressure on you to work harder and longer than was healthy. His not carrying his weight socially or with household chores. His cruelty to you at the end of your life. His immediate search for a new woman. His incomprehensible, and damaging, insensitivity to Lisa's grief and needs since your death.

It helps to see all this in black and white, but how to weigh the good against the bad? They seem pretty equal to me, in his case—he emerges as gray (although a somewhat dark gray), rather than crisp black and white. Your good points, Sara, so overwhelmingly outnumbered your bad that it wasn't anywhere near a close call; you were pure white with just a few daubs of black here and there. Bottom line, I guess, is that there's good and bad in everybody. But the good or the bad is more dominant in some than others—or at least more obvious.

I believe in my heart that Joe deliberately caused you added and unnecessary mental anguish at the very end of your life. I cannot get past that cruelty, and I don't think I ever will be able to. Wasn't it enough that you were *dying*? How much more could anyone be punished? Why tighten the screws? You didn't deserve that. No one does.

There *are* some explanations for Joe's behavior; even I can see that. As much as I hate to admit it, and as wonderful as you were, you were not always the easiest person in the world to live with. Who would know that better than I, who grew up with you and got lost in the shadow of your incredible drive and strong will?

I suspect that's what got you in trouble with Joe, too. Specifically, I believe it was his job situation the last couple of years that was the straw that broke Joe-the-camel's back. When you were first diagnosed, you panicked about your future earning potential and you insisted that Joe get a job. He did, but he hated it—it was a long and miserable commute, and he was not liked or treated well at his place of employment.

You made him stay at the hated job, although you also demanded that he go with you to your every appointment and test, as well as stay home to take care of you on the days when you suffered from chemo side effects. You needed him, and he responded. But all those absences did not endear him to his bosses, no matter the reason. The poor guy was torn between your needs and disapproval and their needs and disapproval. I'm guessing that with his problems in dealing with authority figures, his life was hell. And there would be no way out for him until you died.

You shouldn't have insisted he keep working, Sara. It was too much. Even I told you that at the time. He wasn't strong enough to be all things to all people, especially in a life and death situation. I'm not sure anyone is really strong enough for that.

Still, I have to conclude that I will not be able to forgive Joe, and I doubt that I'll continue any relationship with him once Lisa's grown and gone. My loyalty to you is absolute, and it continues beyond your death. Just as was the case when we were growing up, anyone who hurts you earns my eternal wrath. We are sisters forever.

By the way, that "very special" woman Joe's seeing? Just as I predicted, she's another strong feminist.

*She was no longer wrestling with the grief, but could sit
down with it as a lasting companion and make it a
sharer in her thoughts.*

~ George Eliot

Dear Sara—

I think I'm going to begin to taper off my letter writing to
you, big sister. Now that the weather has finally turned nice I
find myself, more and more, going outside to look up at the sky
and talk aloud to you. I so strongly associate you with Nature
that, at this point anyway, I feel more connected to you by
talking to you outdoors than by writing to you indoors. Every
beautiful day, every colorful butterfly, every graceful bird flying
overhead or gliding down to my feeders reminds me of you and
your great love of the outdoors.

My grief hasn't lessened, but it's changing. I can feel your
loss gradually incorporating into my being, becoming a part of
me. Day by day, at some level, I'm assimilating the reality that
you're gone. I am slowly—and very, very reluctantly—
beginning to adapt to it.

I will try to get out in the world more, I promise you. I think
I need soon to end my days of hiding and hurting, my isolation.

I hope that what I do with the rest of my life will make you proud. I don't know for sure what that will be. A Hospice volunteer? Maybe. That appeals to me very much. There might be a need there for people who are experienced with loss. With all my heart I wish that every single terminally-ill person on earth could be surrounded with the loving care and kindness that you had in your last days. Maybe I could help with that.

Whatever I end up doing, I'll do in honor of you. You taught me and everyone else whose life you touched volumes about compassion, empathy, courage and spirit. This Norman Cousins quote fits: "If something comes to life in others because of you, then you have made an approach to immortality." If I end up helping others, it will be because of you.

I'm still angry with myself for not getting a lock of your hair to put in a mourning ring or brooch to wear always. But I missed that opportunity, and what I've done instead has brought me a surprising amount of comfort. A couple of weeks ago, I bought an oval sterling silver locket, and I had my initials and yours engraved on the back. Inside I have two photos. One is a head shot of you, displaying your radiant smile in all its glory, taken about a year before you died. Opposite that is a photo of you and me together as small children, probably ages three and four, dressed alike. I wear the locket day and night, under my clothing, touching my skin. The chain is just the right length for the locket to nestle near my heart. I remove it only to bathe or shower or swim. It helps to an amazing degree.

There are several things I want you to know absolutely, Sara.

The first is that I will never stop missing you. The second is that you will always be in my heart, even though you're no longer in my life. The third is that I love you—I always have and I always will.

Last and most important, Sara: I won't forget.

All my love,
Anne